Mary Ratcliffe

Einfach besser in Englisch

8. Schuljahr

MANZ VERLAG

Manz Verlag

Lektorat: Harald Kotlarz, Rottenburg
Herstellung: imprint, Zusmarshausen
Illustrationen: Rosanna Pradella, Ludwigsburg
Umschlagkonzept: KünkelLopka, Heidelberg
Umschlagfoto: Fotostudio Maurer, Bamberg
Druck: Finidr s.r.o., Český Těšín

ISBN: 978-3-7863-2203-0

www.manz-verlag.de

Tipps zum Training mit diesem Buch

Mit diesem Buch kannst du die wichtigsten Themen trainieren, die im Englischunterricht des 8. Schuljahres vorkommen. Die Übungen sind einfach, kurz, leicht zu verstehen und sehr abwechslungsreich.

Durch das Inhaltsverzeichnis auf den folgenden beiden Seiten hast du alle Themen im Überblick. So kannst du dir ganz gezielt aussuchen, was du üben willst.

Jedes der insgesamt 43 Kapitel umfasst nur zwei Seiten. Eine kurze Einführung mit Beispielen zeigt dir, worum es auf der Doppelseite geht. Tipps helfen dir zwischendurch beim Lösen einer etwas kniffligeren Aufgabe. Wenn du mit einer Übung fertig bist, kannst du deine Vorschläge mit dem Lösungsteil (ab Seite 106) vergleichen.

Außerdem hast du die Möglichkeit, deine Lernfortschritte mit Hilfe von fünf Tests zu überprüfen (ab Seite 92). Jeder Test fasst die Themen von verschiedenen Kapiteln zusammen. Die zu erreichende Punktzahl ist bei jeder Aufgabe angegeben. Eine Auswertung mit den entsprechenden Notenschritten findest du im Lösungsteil (auf Seite 126).

Du kannst die fünf Tests auch an den Beginn deines Trainings mit diesem Buch stellen: Wenn du die Tests zuerst machst, findest du schnell heraus, mit welchem Thema du Probleme hast.

Dieses Übungsbuch ist die optimale Ergänzung zum Unterricht während des gesamten 8. Schuljahres. Wenn du regelmäßig trainierst, hast du eine gute Basis im Fach Englisch und kannst deine Note stark verbessern.

Inhalt

1 Zustandsverben (stative verbs)

Zustandsverben (*stative verbs*) werden so gut wie immer in der *simple* Form verwendet. Dies sind z. B. *know, belong, believe, contain, understand, need, remember, mean, prefer, seem* (a). Die Verben *see, hear, smell* stehen in der Regel auch nicht in der Verlaufsform, sondern im Infinitiv mit *can / could* (b).
Have (c) und *think* (d) können nur in der Verlaufsform stehen, wenn *think* „überlegen" heißt (nicht „glauben") und wenn *have* eine Tätigkeit (und keinen Besitz) ausdrückt.

a) *Which way is it? Oh, I* ***remember*** *now!*
b) *Listen! I* ***can hear*** *a strange noise.*
c) *Terry* ***had*** *an old house. He* ***was having*** *a bath when the wall collapsed.*
d) *The professor* ***has been thinking*** *about a new invention.*
He thinks it could change the world.

1. Correct the mistakes.

a) I'm sorry, but I'm not understanding you.

___

b) Are you going now? Are you needing anything for the journey?

___

c) They were getting the car out to give us a lift, but we were preferring to walk.

___

d) The boys could hear a car. The sound was seeming to get nearer.

___

e) This ring was belonging to my grandmother but now it's mine.

___

2. **Add *can / can't / could / couldn't and hear / see / smell* to each sentence. The context will tell you which tense and which verb to use.**

Example: Listen! I ___*can hear*___ a strange noise.

a) Can you hear a knocking sound? – No, I ______ anything.

b) Tessa ______ something burning, so she rushed into the kitchen.

c) Anne is funny. She can't smell roses, but she ______ rose-scented soap.

d) Giulia has been blind since she was born. She ______ some things when she was little – candles, for example – but now she's completely blind. She ______ anything.

3. **Underline the right alternative.**

a) I can't go to the door. I'm having / I have a shower.

b) Aaron's teacher is thinking / thinks Aaron will pass the exam.

c) Bob was having / had a new car. When his neighbour looked over the fence, Bob was just having / just had a look at the engine.

d) Sorry, but I'm not thinking / I don't think we can afford a holiday this year.

2 Wiederholung der Zeitformen: *past simple* und *past progressive*

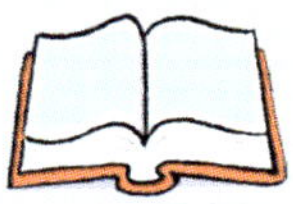

Das ***past progressive*** verwenden wir oft in Verbindung mit *when + simple past* (a) oder *suddenly + simple past* (b). Dem *progressive* geht oft (aber nicht immer) *while* voraus (c). Auch *just* ist ein Signalwort für das *progressive*.

a) ***When*** *the fire alarm* ***went off****, Form 10 BL* ***were just*** *coming out of the video room.*
b) *We were all* ***sitting*** *quietly at our desks.* ***Suddenly*** *the fire alarm* ***went off****.*
c) ***While*** *the teacher* ***was counting*** *the students in the yard, smoke* ***started*** *to pour out of an upstairs window.*

1. Put the verbs in brackets into the *past progressive* or *simple past.*

a) When Petra ____________________ (phone) George to invite him to her party, George ____________________ (just clean) his teeth.

b) He ____________________ (get) into bed when she ____________________ (call) again and asked him to bring a bottle to the party.

c) On the day of the party, George was in a hurry. When he ____________________ (arrive) at the bus stop, the bus ____________________ (just leave).

d) When George ____________________ (ring) Petra's doorbell, nobody heard it. There was loud music and everybody ____________________ (make) a lot of noise.

2. Use the pictures and the words in the box to complete the sentences.

carry • drink • not look • sunbathe • work • write

a) Somebody bumped into Fred while he ______ a full cup of coffee.

b) Somebody stole Duncan's wallet while he ______ .

c) Maria hates having her photo taken, so we took one secretly while she ______ .

d) A thief broke in at the front while we ______ in the back garden.

e) Rob passed a note to Dave while the teacher ______ on the board.

3 Wiederholung der Zeitformen: present perfect simple und progressive

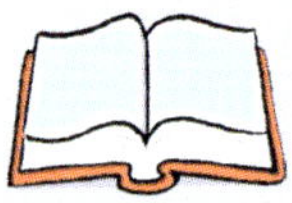

Die Verlaufsform *(progressive)* des *present perfect* wird so gebildet:
have / has + been + -ing. Damit wird entweder der Zeitraum betont (a, b) oder der Zustand einer Person erklärt (c, d).
Die Zustandsverben (*stative verbs* ➞ Kapitel 1) stehen nie im *progressive* (e).

a) *Those workers are very slow.* ***They've been mending the fence since nine o'clock this morning*** *and they still haven't finished.*
b) ***Mr Robinson has been driving around London for ten years*** *and he still gets lost.*
c) *Your clothes are covered in paint! What* ***have you been doing?***
d) *You look hot. – Yes,* ***I've been baking*** cakes.
e) *Tom and Sue* ***have known*** *each other since they were children.*

1. Complete the sentences with *since + a point in time or for + a period of time*. Write true sentences about yourself. For sentence (d) choose your own verb, e.g. *going out with Kim, playing the trumpet, riding …*

a) I've been living in our house ______________________________

b) I've been going to my present school ______________________________

c) I've been packing my own school bag ______________________________

d) I've been ______________________________

2. Put the verb into the present perfect simple or progressive.

a) The twins ______________________________ (play) the piano since they were six years old.

b) ____________________ they ever ____________________ (play) Beethoven's 'Moonlight Sonata'?

c) Adrian is practising now. He ______________________________ (not practise) for very long.

d) He ______________________________ (just do) some finger exercises and now he's starting the piece by Bach.

e) Recently the twins ______________________________ (start) playing duets together.

3. **Find an explanation for these sentences.**

Example: Your hands are black. (repair) – ***I've been repairing my bike.***

Eines der Verben ist ein *stative verb*, das nicht in der Verlaufsform stehen darf.

Tipp

a) You look tired. (work hard)

– Yes, ____ .

b) Your voice sounds funny. (shout)

– Yes, I went to a football match this afternoon. ____________________

____ .

c) What's the matter? Why do you look so worried? (just remember something)

____ .

It's Pat's birthday today and I haven't sent him a card.

d) You've got flour in your hair. (make bread)

– Have I? ____

e) What has the baby been doing? Look at her face! (try to feed herself again)

– Yes, I know. ____

4 Wiederholung der Zeitformen: will-future und going to-future

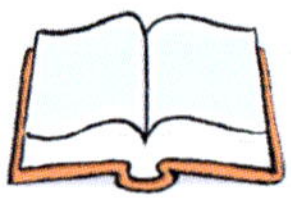

Das Hilfsverb ***will*** wird für Angebote (a), Versprechen (b) und Vermutungen (c) oder spontane Entscheidungen verwendet. ***Going to*** bezieht sich auf begründete Informationen, die aus Plänen (d), sicherer Information (e) oder Offensichtlichkeiten (f) bestehen.

a) *That bag looks heavy.* ***I'll carry*** *it for you.*
b) *I'm sorry.* ***I won't do*** *it again.*
c) *Grandad has had his operation.*
They'll probably let *him out on Tuesday.*
d) ***Are you going to phone*** *Helen tonight?*
e) *Did you hear that announcement?*
The train is going to be *ten minutes late.*
f) ***It's going to take*** *years to replace all the damage from the earthquake.*

1. Make sentences with *will*.

Example:
probably / Dennis / not win / the race

Dennis probably won't win the race.

a) probably / the bus / be late

____

b) you / open / the window / please?

____

c) The letter / probably / not arrive / until Friday

____

d) what / he / do?

Poor Tom! ______________________________

2. Make sentences with *going to*.

Example:
you / invite / Sandy / too?

Are you going to invite Sandy, too?

a) I / certainly / not / go out in this weather

______

b) it / rain

______

c) where / Anne / have her baby?

______

d) which / piece / you / play?
You play the Mozart and the Bach equally well. ______

______

3. Make sentences with *will* or *going to*.

Signalwörter für *will* sind: *sure, probably, expect, hope, think.* Tipp

a) Don't worry. I'm sure ______ (it / be) all right.

b) What did the weather forecast say? ______ (it / rain)?

c) Do you think ______ (you / pass) the exam?

d) We ______ (probably / not / have) time to go to the museum.

e) Ethel says she ______ (not / send) any Christmas cards this year.

f) The girls are having an overnight party. ______ (they / watch) films all night – at least, that's what they say.

5 Wiederholung der Zeitformen: simple past und present perfect

Das ***present perfect*** bezieht sich immer auf die Gegenwart, auch wenn das Ereignis weiter zurückliegt (a, b). Signalwörter sind *just, recently, over the past … (days, years), since*. Das ***simple past*** beschreibt eine Handlung in der Vergangenheit, die keinen Bezug mehr zur Gegenwart hat, auch wenn die Handlung nicht lange zurückliegt (c, d). Signalwörter sind Zeitangaben, z. B. *last (week), ago, at (two o'clock), when …*

a) *Grandad* ***has had*** *another operation on his heart. He's still in hospital.*
b) *Poor old Grandad. He* ***has had*** *six operations over the past twenty years.*
c) *The first one* ***was*** *before I was born.*
d) *We* ***went*** *to see him this afternoon. He* ***seemed*** *quite cheerful.*

1. Put the verbs into the *simple past.*

In 1620 a group of people who ______________________ (not agree) with the Church of England ______________________ (leave) England for North America. They ______________________ (want) religious freedom and ______________________ (think) – rightly – that they would find it in the New World.

These people ______________________ (be) called the Pilgrims, and their ship ______________________ (be) called the Mayflower. They ______________________ (make) a mistake in navigation and ______________________ (not land) in Virginia as they had planned. They ______________________ (come) to Plymouth Rock instead, and ______________________ (start) a new colony there. They ______________________ (survive) because an Indian who ______________________ (speak) English ______________________ (teach) them how to catch turkeys. Later turkey ______________________ (become) the traditional meal at Thanksgiving.

2. **Put the verbs into the *present perfect.***

Ever since the 16th century, America ______________________ (be) the destination of millions of settlers and immigrants. It ______________________ (always have) a reputation for liberty and opportunity. And it is true that over the years, a lot of immigrants ______________________ (make) their fortunes there. Many people ______________________ (write) books and articles about the phenomenon of America, or the United States, as it ______________________ (be) called since its independence.

3. **Put the verbs into the *simple past* or the *present perfect.***

Aaron's parents ______________________ (come) to America from Germany in 1934. At that time they ______________________ (not possess) much money, but they ______________________ (manage) to set up a small business. Since then there ______________________ (be) ups and downs in the business, but at the moment it's doing well. Aaron and his brother ______________________ (take over) the firm from their parents in the 1960s and recently they ______________________ (make) some changes. Profits ______________________ (rise) in the last few years. When their parents ______________________ (start) the business all those years ago they ______________________ (think) it might be a success, but they ______________________ (not know) for sure. Now they do.

6 Aktiv und Passiv I

Für die **Bildung des Passivs** benötigt man eine Form von ***to be*** *(am, is, are, was, were, will be)* und das ***past participle*** *(eaten, run, done, called)* des Verbs.
Ist es wichtig, wer etwas getan hat, so erwähnt man es durch den ***by-agent.***

a) *The Pilgrims* ***called*** *their ship the Mayflower.*
b) *The ship* ***was called*** *the Mayflower (by the Pilgrims).*
c) *Thousands of people* ***eat*** *hamburgers every day.*
d) *Thousands of hamburgers* ***are eaten*** *every day (by a lot of people).*

1. Make these passive sentences into active ones, keeping the same tense.

Tipp Nimm den *by-agent* als Subjekt des Aktivsatzes.

Example:
The thief was caught by the police.

The police caught the thief. ______

a) The old people's home has been decorated by volunteers.

______

b) The two girls were driven home by a neighbour.

______

c) I expect that the wedding dress will be made by the bride's mother.

I expect that ______

2. Make these active sentences into passive ones. The agent *(someone, people, the police etc.)* 'disappears' from the passive sentence.

Example:
Someone found the missing guinea pig.

The missing guinea pig was found.

a) The police usually catch criminals eventually.

Criminals ______________________________

b) We only use this silver spoon on special occasions.

____

c) Someone took this photo last Christmas.

____

3. Underline the correct alternative.

a) The dog gives / is given one meal a day.

b) The cat gets / is got one meal a day, too.

c) These shoes have never worn / have never been worn.

d) Has that cake eaten / been eaten already?

e) Only the top two leaves of the tea plant pick / are picked.

f) We watched / were watched the match against England last night.

g) The match watched / was watched by thousands of viewers.

h) Have the candles lit / been lit yet?

i) I stopped / was stopped on the way to Augsburg last week.
It was a routine police check.

j) Later on I stopped / was stopped for a coffee.

7 Aktiv und Passiv II

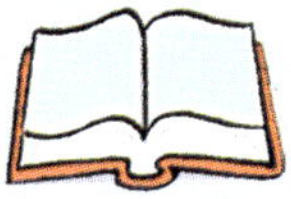

Hier hast du Gelegenheit, Form und Satzbau von Aktiv- und Passivsätzen zu üben. Achte auch auf den Inhalt des Satzes: ein Tisch wird gebaut, er kann nicht selber bauen (a). Katzen werden in der Regel nicht gegessen (b), sondern sie fressen.

a) *This table **was made** in the nineteenth century.*
b) *The cat **eats** in the evening.*

1. These sentences contain typical 'German' mistakes. Make them into passives. Mind the tenses!

Example:
The smaller car drives my mother.

The smaller car is driven by my mother.

a) The magazine write the pupils.

____

b) This house built my grandfather.

____

c) The voice-over in the film did a boy at our school.

____

d) The steps clean the children.

____

2. Put the verb in brackets into the active or passive form of the simple present.

a) The dog ______________ (take) for a walk every morning.

b) Jane and Sally ______________ (usually / cook) in the evening.

c) Exams ______________________ (often / do) at the end of term.

d) The Bible ______________________ (read) all over the world.

e) Bread dough ______________________ (rise) if you leave it in a warm place.

3. **Put the verb in brackets into the active or passive form of the simple past.**

a) Joanna's handbag ______________________ (steal) at a disco.

b) When we opened the door, it ______________________ (make) a strange noise.

c) Robert ______________________ (give) a talk to the rest of the class yesterday.

d) The teacher liked the talk, and Robert ______________________ (give) a good mark for his talk.

4. **Make actives or passives out of these auxiliary / verb combinations.**

a) The work ______________________ (must / do) quickly.

b) Quick, hide! We ______________________ (mustn't / see).

c) You ______________________ (needn't / finish) the homework by tomorrow.

d) All the computers ______________________ (should / switch off) before you leave.

e) The last person to leave ______________________ (must / lock) the door.

8 Passivsätze mit zwei Objekten

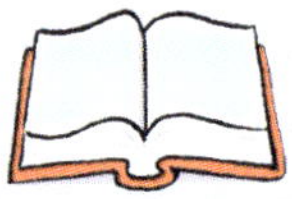

Ein Satz mit einem direkten und einem indirekten Objekt kann im Passiv auf zweierlei Art ausgedrückt werden, je nachdem, worauf die Betonung gelegt wird.

The president *gave the boy a cup.*

A cup *was given to the boy (by the president).*

The boy *was given a cup (by the president).*

1. Write the active sentence for these passives. Use *they* if there is no by-agent.

Example:
The two girls were given another chance.

They gave the two girls another chance.

a) I have been promised a new bike by my parents.

___

b) We were told a lot of stories which we didn't believe.

___

c) I hope my dad will be offered the job.

___

d) Have you been given more time for the project?

---

e) I've been given your address by Susan Adams.

---

2. **Now try the same thing the other way round. You don't need a by-agent for *they* or *somebody*.**

Example:
They gave the two girls another chance.

The two girls were given another chance.

a) Mandy's parents have promised her a trekking holiday.

Mandy

b) They have sent us a brochure about adventure holidays.

---

c) Yesterday somebody offered Tim and Susan free tickets for the circus.

---

d) At the museum they showed us some old film sets.

---

e) Somebody showed the girls some photographs of the race.

---

9 Passiv bei Objekten mit Präposition

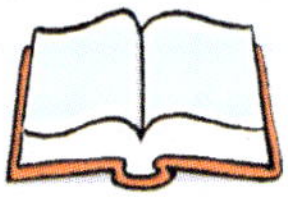

Ein Objekt mit Präposition wird im Passiv an den Anfang des Satzes gestellt.
Dabei bleibt die Präposition hinter dem Verb, wandert also nicht mit dem Nomen zum Satzanfang wie im Deutschen.

Vergleiche die beiden Sprachen:
*They haven't fought **in this boxing ring** for two weeks.*

➠ ***This boxing ring** hasn't been fought **in** for two weeks.*

⬇

In diesem Boxring wurde seit zwei Wochen nicht mehr gekämpft.

1. Underline the subject, and the preposition which belongs to it, in each of these passive sentences.

Example:
The chairs have been swept under.

a) The Queen is often talked about.

b) Vegetarians will be cooked for separately.

c) Churches aren't usually danced in.

2. When Matthew's parents came back from a weekend away, they found that their house had been used for a party. Put the parts of the sentences into the right order.

Example: had been / with / the computer / played

The computer had been played with.

a) slept / in / hadn't been / Matthew's bed

___

b) on / the table / danced / had been

___

c) on / trodden (treten auf) / had been / the flower beds

____

d) the garden hose / with / played / had been

____

3. **Make passive sentences.**

Mr and Mrs Smith and their little daughter, Susie, shared their house with a ghost. People said they were crazy to go on living there. It really was sometimes a bit of a nuisance (etwas lästig). He ate off their plates when they weren't looking. He played with Susie's dolls in the night. He slept in her bed during the day. He trod on the clean floor and muddy footprints appeared. He drank out of the milk bottles in the fridge. On the other hand, he was often helpful. He swept under the cupboards while they were out. He looked after the plants when they were away on holiday. On the whole, they were glad that they had a ghost.
What do the Smiths say?

Example:

Our plates ***have been eaten off.***

a) Poor Susie! Her dolls ______________________

b) And her bed ______________________

c) Look at the floor. It ______________________

d) This milk bottle ______________________

e) Oh, that's nice. The cupboards ______________________

f) Goodness! We've been away for a week, and the plants are fine.

They must ______________________

10 Past perfect I

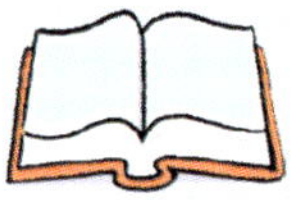

Um eine Abfolge vergangener Ereignisse zu erzählen, verwenden wir *past tense* (a). Wird ein Ereignis oder eine Handlung erwähnt, die vor dieser Abfolge lag, geschieht das mit dem ***past perfect*** (b).

a) *Tom **got up** at six o'clock. He **made** a pot of tea and **waited** for six minutes.*
b) *It didn't take long to make the tea, because he **had prepared** everything the night before.*

1. **This text starts with Sunday afternoon. Underline the verbs for everything which happened before that.**

On Sunday afternoon Tim was very tired. He had had a busy weekend. He had played in a football match, which his team had lost. Then he had done his English homework. On Sunday morning he had taken the dog for a long walk. So on Sunday he went to bed early and slept for nine hours.

a) Which tense is used for the events which happened before Sunday afternoon?

☐ simple past ☐ past perfect

b) Which tense is used for the events which happened after Sunday afternoon?

☐ simple past ☐ past perfect

2. **This text starts at quarter to eight on Monday morning.**

a) Underline the verbs for everything that happened before that.

Tim arrived at school at quarter to eight on Monday morning. He had forgotten to do his maths homework at the weekend. David had arrived before Tim, and Tim asked if he could copy the homework. David said that was all right, and Tim started writing.

b) Which tense is used for the events which happened before the event in the first sentence?

☐ simple past ☐ past perfect

3. **Use two different colours to underline the things which happened a) before and b) after the event in the first sentence.**

Suddenly Tim heard a noise behind him. The maths teacher had quietly walked up to him, and Tim hadn't noticed. Then Tim looked round and saw him. Tim didn't know what to say. But the teacher just smiled and went to his desk.

4. **Study each mini-text and decide which event happened first, which next and so on. Then put the letters in chronological order.**

Example:

A: Rico watched an American film with two friends.
B: He had seen it twice already,
C: so by the end, he was really bored. B – A – C

The order is B (Rico watched the film twice), A (Rico and his friends watched the film; for Rico the third time), C (by the end of the film, Rico was bored).

a) A: Susie came home at half past two, but
B: she had left her coat at school, so
C: she had to go back for it. ☐ – ☐ – ☐

b) A: Daniel ordered a vegetarian pizza.
B: When it arrived, he complained, because
C: they had put fish on it. ☐ – ☐ – ☐

c) A: Sarah and Pete decided to cycle to Cheddar.
B: They got lost, because
C: they hadn't studied the map very carefully. ☐ – ☐ – ☐

d) A: Pete asked his dad if he could borrow the car, but
B: his dad wouldn't lend it to him because
C: Pete had only just passed his driving test. ☐ – ☐ – ☐

11 Past perfect II

Das ***past perfect*** wird für Handlungen verwendet, die vor der eigentlichen Handlung lagen (a).
Das *past perfect* wird auch in untergeordneten Nebensätzen mit *after / when* verwendet (b).

a) *Alex* ***washed*** *his face, then he* ***went*** *into the kitchen.*
His mother ***had left*** *a packet of sandwiches on the table for him.*

b) *After Alex* ***had made*** *some tea he found that there were no clean cups in the cupboard.*

1. Here is a little story. Read it and use the past perfect to change the order.

a) For years the people at Oakland old folks' home wanted a fence around the garden.
b) Topple and Co. were asked to make a fence for them.
c) They didn't plan the fence very well.
d) They made a bad mistake.
e) The builders finished the fence.
f) They found that they couldn't get their lorry out.

b) – a)

Topple and Co ***were asked to make a fence*** ______ at Oakland old folks' home, because ***the people there*** ______

______

______

d) – c)

They ______ because they

______

e) – f)

After they ______, they

______

2. Barney isn't very clever. Explain these jokes to him with a past perfect.

a) Noah and his wife were talking about their animals. Noah said: 'Didn't we have two turkeys when we started?'
His wife answered: 'Yes, we did, but – well, it is Christmas …'

Well you see, Barney, there was only one turkey because

Mrs Noah

b) James bought a parrot for his grandmother for Christmas. She often felt lonely, so James found a parrot which could talk, and it was very expensive. After Christmas he asked her: 'Did you like the parrot?'
'Yes, dear,' she answered. 'It was delicious.'

Do you get it, Barney? She said it was delicious because she

c) James had the same sort of problem the next Christmas. This time he asked his grandmother what she wanted, just to be on the safe side. She said she often felt cold, and asked him to bring a good big sack of firewood. But James thought that was a poor Christmas present, and bought her a large antique rocking chair instead. A week later he asked how she liked it.
'Great!' she said. 'I felt really warm for three days.'

You see, Barney, she said she had felt warm because she

12 Wiederholung der Zeitformen: *past progressive* und *past perfect (progressive)*

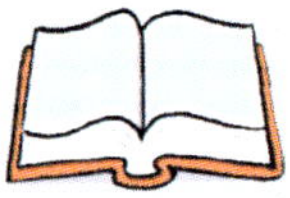

Das ***past progressive*** drückt einen Handlungsverlauf aus, der eine Zeitspanne unmittelbar vor (a) oder während (c) einer anderen, zentralen Handlung ausfüllt und noch nicht zu Ende gebracht wurde. Für eine Handlung, die schon beendet ist, wird das *past perfect verwendet* (b, d). Das ***past perfect progressive*** wird ähnlich dem *present perfect progressive (have been doing)* verwendet, außer dass die Erzählzeit Vergangenheit ist.

a) *When the lights went out we **were having** a game of chess. We had to stop playing.*
b) *When the lights went out we **had just had** a game of chess. James was happy because he **had won**.*
c) *When the storm broke, I **was just coming** home. I got wet.*
d) *When the storm broke, I **had just come** home. I was lucky.*
e) *Dave **was** thirsty because he **had been running**.*

1. Tick the box for the right context sentence (like the sentence *I got wet* in c) above).

a) When the phone rang I had just read an article about Thailand.
☐ I never finished reading it.
☐ The last sentence was very long and complicated.

b) When I got up at seven thirty, Alice was using the bathroom.
☐ I had to wait.
☐ It smelled of roses.

c) When Pete came out of the house on his way to the station, his dad was mending the car.
☐ He asked Pete to fetch him a spanner.
☐ He offered Pete a lift to the station.

d) When we arrived at the party, John had already left.
☐ We had a chat with him in the doorway.
☐ We were sorry about missing him.

2. Put the verb into the *past progressive* or the *past perfect*.

a) Alex ______ (write) a letter so she put it in an envelope.

b) She ______ (look for) a stamp when she suddenly remembered that she ______ (use) the last stamp the day before.

c) Her mother ______ (just / go) out of the house, so she asked her to buy some more stamps while she was out.

d) Her mother arrived back an hour later, but unfortunately, she ______ (forget) the stamps.

e) Alex went out and bought some stamps herself, because the letter was urgent and her friend ______ (wait) for it.

3. Underline the right form of the verb: *past perfect progressive* or *past progressive*.

a) Lucy lay down on a bench and had a drink because she had been running / was running.

b) Poor Dave had bad dreams because he had been watching / was watching a horror film.

c) Theresa couldn't go to the phone because she had been bathing / was bathing the baby.

d) The chair I had been sitting on / was sitting on collapsed under my uncle's great weight.

13 Bedingungssätze Typ I und Typ II

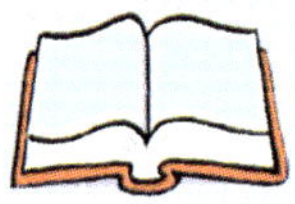

Der **Bedingungssatz Typ I** (a, b) bezieht sich auf ein mögliches, aber unsicheres Ereignis in der Zukunft, während der **Typ II** (c, d) ein vorgestelltes Ereignis in der Gegenwart oder ein höchst unwahrscheinliches Ereignis in der Zukunft ausdrückt.
Anders als im Deutschen darf im ***if-clause*** kein *will* bzw. *would* erscheinen.
Die Wendung *if I was* existiert neben *if I were*.

a) *We haven't got an umbrella, so* ***if it rains, we'll get wet.***
b) ***If you get there early, wait for me*** *inside the building.*
c) ***If the Queen invited me*** *to her next garden party* ***I would buy*** a new suit.
d) ***If the car was here I would offer*** *you a lift; but I've lent my car to my son.*

1. Type I conditionals. Fill in the if-clause, using the verb from the second sentence. One of the verbs is negative.

Example:

*If I remember*_______________, I'll phone you. I probably will remember.

a) ________ *Sandra* ____________________, will you give her this message? She said she was going to phone this afternoon.

b) ________ *that book* ____________________, I won't be able to use it for my project. I hope it will come soon.

c) ________ *I* __________________________ to mend my bike, we'll go for a cycle ride. I think I will manage to mend it.

2. Type II conditionals for unreal situations in the present. Fill in the if-clause, using the but-sentence for the information you need.

Example:

If I had a play station, ______ I would play games on it all night. But I haven't got a play station.

a) ______________________________, I would give lots of money to the poor. But I'm not rich.

b) ______ *Steve* ______________________ so much, he would be a lot healthier. But unfortunately he smokes like a chimney.

c) ______ *this train* ______________________, it would take hours to get to London. But luckily it's an express. It doesn't stop at every station.

3. Type II conditionals for unlikely situations in the future. Use the second sentence for the information you need.

Example:

If Victoria went to South America ______ this summer she could learn Spanish very quickly. But she probably won't go to South America.

a) ______________________________, I would give a lot of it to the homeless. But I probably won't win the jackpot.

b) What would you do ______________________________? I know you'll probably never see a ghost, of course.

c) ______________________________, we wouldn't have any lessons for weeks and weeks. But I don't suppose the school will ever catch fire.

14 Bedingungssätze Typ III

Bedingungssätze des **Typs III** schildern Handlungen, die nicht geschehen sind oder sich nur in der Fantasie abspielen. Anders als Typ II bezieht sich Typ III auf die Vergangenheit. Der Hauptsatz kann sich auf die Gegenwart (a) (*would* + Verb) oder die Vergangenheit (b) (*would have* + Verb) beziehen.

a) *Joan has a French boyfriend.* ***If she had done French*** *at school, she* ***would be able to*** *communicate with his parents.* ***But she didn't do French,*** *she did Latin.*

b) ***If we had written all our postcards on the first day*** *of the holiday, they* ***would have arrived*** *before we got back.* ***But we didn't write them on the first day,*** *we wrote them on the last day.*

1. Write the if-clause for these sentences. Use the underlined elements for the information you need. The would-clause is in the present.

Example:
Sandra spent a year at school in France.

If she hadn't spent a year in France,
she wouldn't be able to speak such good French now.

a) Richard lived in Italy when he was younger.

____,
he wouldn't know so much about making pizzas.

b) Wendy bought an electric piano last year.

____,
he wouldn't be able to practise every day.

c) Ronny and Arnie didn't put their coats on when they went out in the snow.

____,
they wouldn't be ill now.

2. **Use the underlined elements to make an if-clause. This time the would-clause is in the past.**

a) I studied very hard for the exam.

______________________________,
I would have failed it.

b) Luckily, I went to the party.

______________________________,
I wouldn't have met Michele.

c) You didn't look under the doormat.

______________________________,
you would have found the key.

3. **Finish the sentences with a *would have / wouldn't have*-clause, using the ideas in the boxes.**

a) go | to | party

If I hadn't been ill,

____

b) the boys | wake | up

If the alarm clock had gone off,

____

c) miss | our connection

If the train hadn't been late, we

____

d) catch | the plane

Poor Andrew. If there hadn't been such a bad traffic jam on the motorway,

he ______________________________

15 Indirekte Rede (reported speech)

Wenn wir berichten, was jemand sagt, dann müssen wir darauf achten, notwendige Änderungen bei Personalpronomen durchzuführen (a). Die Zeitformen bleiben gleich, wenn das *reporting verb* (z. B. *says*) in einer Zeitform des Präsens steht. Ortsangaben müssen gelegentlich angepasst werden (b).

a)	*Alan:*	***I'll** send **you** a postcard from **my** uncle's farm in Australia.*
	Philip:	*Alan says **he'll** send **me** a postcard from **his** uncle's farm in Australia.*
b)	*Alan's postcard:*	*It's very hot **here**.*
	Philip:	*He says it's very hot **there**.*

1. Some parts of Text A are underlined. Underline the same parts in Text B.

Text A: Part of a letter from Alan's uncle in Australia to Alan's mother in England.

... I'm sure Alan would like to visit me on my farm again. He can come out here next summer if you agree. Peter can come, too, if he wants to. I'll meet them both at the airport. I tried to phone you last week but I couldn't get through. ...

Text B: Alan is telling his friend Philip about the letter.

See this? It's a letter to my mum from my uncle in Australia. He says he's sure that I would like to visit him on his farm again. He says I can go out there next summer if my mum agrees, and that Peter can come too if he wants to. He says he'll meet us both at the airport. He tried to phone my mum the week before, but he couldn't get through.

2. **Can you find out what Alan actually says?**

Alan says he sometimes visits his uncle in Australia, and that his uncle meets them in Melbourne. He says that they have a long drive to his sheep farm. He also says that I've met his uncle, but I don't remember that.

Alan: *I sometimes visit my uncle* in Australia.

__________ in Melbourne.

Then __________ to his sheep farm.

__________ uncle.

Don't you remember?

3. **Now it's your turn to report.**

Alan: We have great fun on the farm. We often ride our uncle's horses. We ride round the fence with him. I'll send you a postcard from Australia, but I don't know when it will arrive.

Alan says *they have great fun* on the farm. He says __________ horses, and that __________ round the fence with him.

He says __________ a postcard from Australia, but __________ when it will get here.

16 Reported speech in der Vergangenheit

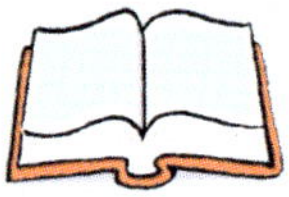

Wenn das *reporting verb* im ***past*** (z. B. *said, told, wrote*) steht, müssen die Zeitformen der direkten Rede zurückgesetzt werden ***(backshift of tenses)***:

present ➠ *past*
past ➠ *past perfect*
present perfect ➠ *past perfect*
will ➠ *would*

Dies gilt für die einfachen Zeiten und die Verlaufsformen gleichermaßen. Orts- und Zeitangaben müssen ebenfalls angepasst werden *(tomorrow, here)*.

Alan's postcard from Australia:
*We **are** having a great time **here.** We **arrived yesterday evening.***
*Philip: I had a postcard from Alan yesterday. He wrote that he **was** having a great time **there**, and that they **had arrived the evening before**.*

1. This text is written in reported speech. What did Alan actually say?

Philip: Alan phoned me yesterday from Australia. He said something terrible had happened there. He told me that his uncle was in hospital and he couldn't take them to the airport, so they would probably miss their plane.

Alan: Hello, Phil. It's me. I'm still in Australia. Something terrible

____

____

in hospital, and he ______________________________

take us to the airport, so ______________________________

probably miss ______________________________

2. **Now you can put the conversation into reported speech.**

Alan: I can tell you exactly what happened, but it will take a long time, because it's a long story. Do you want to hear it?

Philip: Well, I do, but your uncle will have to pay a lot for this phone call. Tell me when you get home.

Alan: Okay. Anyway, he had a bad accident yesterday. He has broken his leg and he won't be able to ride a horse for a few weeks. I want to stay here with Peter, so that we can help my uncle on the farm, but I don't think my mother will let us.

A few days later, Philip is telling his friends about the phone call.

He said ______________________ exactly what ______________

__________, but that it ____________________________________

a long time, because it ______________________ a long story. He

asked me if I ________________ to hear it. I said I ____________,

but that ____________________ uncle ___________________

_______________ pay a lot for the phone call. I told him to tell me

when ______________________ home. Then Alan said that his uncle

______________________ a bad accident ___________________

He said ____ his

leg and that he ______________________ to ride a horse for a few

weeks. He said he wanted to stay ___________________ with Peter, so

that ______________________ help ________________ uncle on

the farm, but he said he ______________________ his mother ______

____

17 Fragen in der indirekten Rede

Eine **indirekte Frage** weist die gleiche Struktur auf wie ein Aussagesatz: Subjekt – Verb / Hilfsverb. Der Nebensatz passt sich der Zeitform des Hauptverbs an, ist das Verb also im *past*, werden die Zeitformen zurückgesetzt (b).

a) *I don't know what* ***they are*** *doing in the park.*
b) *I asked her who* ***she was*** *going to visit.*
c) *Can you tell me when* ***this bus leaves?***

1. What's the question?

Example: I asked my mum what she was doing.

What are you doing, Mum?

a) We asked the new boy, Paul, how old he was.

____

b) I asked them where I could leave my bags.

____

c) The kids didn't know what 'weather' meant.

____

d) Mr Lee is going to find out when the holidays start.

____

e) They wanted to know where the ticket office was.

____

f) They asked us when the next ferry left for the Isle of Wight.

____

2. Now it's your turn to complete the indirect question. Don't forget the backshift of tenses (c, e) and change of pronouns (e).

Example: Where are you going tomorrow, Tom?

Tom, I want to know where you are going tomorrow.

a) Tom, where have you put your bike? Tom, I want to know

____

b) Excuse me, how old is this church? Excuse me, can you tell me

______________________________, please?

c) We said 'how much does this pullover cost?' We asked the assistant

____

d) Where can we swim? I'm going to ask that old man

____

e) They said 'what have you done with the money?' They asked me

____

18 Indirekte Fragen mit dem to-Infinitiv

Die **indirekte Frage,** die aus *to* + Infinitiv besteht, entspricht einem deutschen Nebensatz mit „soll".

a) ***We****'re wondering what* ***to do*** *with the bikes.*
b) ***Frances*** *didn't know where* ***to park*** *her car.*
Das Subjekt kommt nur einmal vor, statt zweimal wie im Deutschen:
Wir wissen nicht, was **wir** …
Frances wusste nicht, wo **sie** …

1. Make direct questions with *shall* from these indirect questions with *to.*

Example: The children didn't know how to get to the island.

How shall we get to the island?

a) We don't know where to go.

b) Sarah didn't know what to wear.

c) I wasn't sure when to leave.

d) Philip couldn't decide which basketball to buy.

e) We didn't know which way to go.

f) Lucy has won a huge teddy bear, and she doesn't know what to do with it.

g) She'd like to give it to someone, but she doesn't know who to give it to.

2. **Put the words into the right order to make an indirect question with to-infinitive.**

a) know – to – doesn't – do – what – Sarah

____

b) I want the card to get there on her birthday.
when – don't – post – I – know – it – to

____

c) Both shirts are nice.
one – buy – I – which – know – to – don't

____

3. **Now it's your turn to form indirect questions with the to-infinitive.**

a) What shall I cook? – I asked Granny ______________________.

b) How do you repair a bike chain?

Bob asked Steve ______________________.

c) Which animals should we feed?

We wanted to know ______________________.

d) How often should we water the plants?

We weren't sure ______________________.

e) How do I switch the computer off?

He didn't even know ______________________.

f) Oh no! What shall I do?

He doesn't know ______________________ in an emergency.

19 Indirekte Aufforderungen mit dem to-Infinitiv

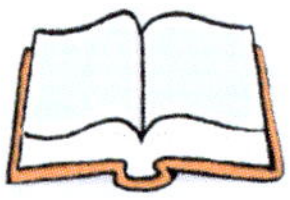

Wir können einen Befehl (a) oder eine Anweisung indirekt berichten, indem wir das Gesagte mit dem Hauptverb *tell* (auch *order, warn, instruct, ask*) einleiten, und die Anweisungen als Infinitiv mit *to* wiedergeben. Weil das Verb im Infinitiv ist, spielt *backshift of tenses* keine Rolle, aber Pronomen müssen geändert werden (b). Bei der Verneinung steht *not* vor dem *to-Infinitiv* (c).

a) ***Get up,*** *please.* ➠ *Mum* ***told me to get up,*** *but I didn't.*
b) *Will* ***you*** *put the oven on at 12.15, please?* ➠ *Mum* ***asked me to put*** *the oven on at 12.15.*
c) *Don't worry.* ➠ *They told me* ***not to worry.***

1. Write the direct version of these indirect commands.

Example: The recipe tells you to steam the mixture.

Steam the mixture.

Tipp

Das Ausrufezeichen (!) ist für geschriebene Anweisungen im Englischen **nicht** üblich und würde als unhöflich gelten. Eher wird *please* angehängt.

a) They asked us to wait.

____

b) At the airport we were told to empty our pockets.

____

c) Susan told Tom to phone her at six o'clock.

Will you ______________________________

2. Write the direct version of these indirect, negative requests.

a) There were notices all over the place telling people not to smoke.

____

b) Mum told me not to forget Dad's birthday.

____

c) I was going to get a chair for Mrs Pearson, but she told me not to bother.

____

3. **Now it's your turn to write the indirect version. Don't forget to change the pronouns where necessary. This is what the English teacher says:**

a) Don't waste time.

b) Tom, stop playing with your ruler.

c) Put it away.

d) Now, Group A, turn to page 52. Group B, turn to page 106. You'll find some information for a dialogue.

e) Work with a partner from the other group and follow the instructions.

f) Don't look at your partner's information.

g) Look up any new words in the dictionary.

Example: Get your English books out.

Mrs Parr told us ***to get our English books out.***

This is what Tom tells his sister later, on the way home.

a) She told us ______________________________.

b) Then she warned me ______________________________.

c) She told me ______________________________.

d) Then she ______________________________,

and Group B ______________________________.

She said we would find some information for a dialogue.

e) She asked us ______________________________

f) She told us ______________________________

g) She ______________________________

20 Gerundium und Infinitiv I

Nach einer Präposition steht immer das **Gerundium** (a). Auch nach den Verben *suggest, avoid, enjoy, finish, miss, practise* und anderen steht das Gerundium (b). Die Verben *decide, invite, want, expect, tell* werden mit dem **Infinitiv** mit *to* gebraucht (c). Nach den Verben *like, love, prefer, hate, begin, start, continue* kann ohne großen Bedeutungsunterschied entweder Gerundium (d) oder Infinitiv (e) stehen. Nach *would like, would prefer* steht der Infinitiv (f).

a) *He **insisted on putting** the lights on, although the sun was shining.*
b) *The trainee nurses have to **practise giving** injections.*
c) *Simon **invited** Freda **to share** his pizza.*
d) *When did the group **begin planning** the project?*
e) When did the group ***begin to plan** the project?*
f) ***Would** you like **to sit down?***

1. Gerund + preposition. Translate into English, using the following phrases.

apologize for — be interested in — insist on — thank (you) for

a) Ich interessiere mich fürs Reiten.

I'm ______________________________

b) Die Lehrerin besteht darauf, alle Fenster geschlossen zu halten.

____

c) Tom und seine Freunde entschuldigten sich dafür, dass sie so viel Lärm gemacht hatten.

____

d) Danke, dass du auf mich gewartet hast!

____

2. Give an infinitive or a gerund for the verb in brackets.

a) We decided ________ (go) to the castle by bike.

b) Andy suggested ________ (take) a picnic.

c) Jessie didn't have a bike, so Phil invited her ________ (ride) on his crossbar.

d) Then Rob offered ________ (lend) her his mother's bike.

e) By the time they had finished ________ (discuss) the problem it was nearly too late to start out.

f) In the end Jessie said she would like ________ (borrow) Rob's mother's bike.

g) They wanted ________ (be) back by six.

h) They didn't want to miss ________ (see) the next episode of 'Eastenders'.

i) When they finally started out, they all enjoyed ________ (ride) through the beautiful countryside.

j) Jessie had always avoided ________ (go) on cycle tours, and was surprised that it was such fun.

21 Gerundium und Infinitiv II

Bei *like, love, hate, prefer, begin, continue* ist der Bedeutungsunterschied zwischen Gerund und Infinitiv gering (a). Bei *stop, remember, forget* gibt es dagegen einen wesentlichen Bedeutungsunterschied (b–g).
Beim Infinitiv ist die Handlung zur Erzählzeit noch unerledigt.
Beim Gerund ist die Handlung zur Erzählzeit schon geschehen.

a) *continue singing / to sing*	weitersingen
b) *stop doing sth.*	aufhören, etw. zu machen
c) *stop to do sth.*	halten, um etw. zu machen
d) *remember doing sth.*	sich daran erinnern etw. gemacht zu haben
e) *remember to do sth.*	daran denken, etw. (noch) zu erledigen
f) *forget doing sth.*	vergessen, etw. gemacht zu haben
g) *forget to do sth.*	nicht daran denken, etw. (noch) zu machen

1. Complete the German translations. In most cases you will need one of these phrases: *weiterhin, gern, sehr gern, lieber, sehr ungern.*

a) Luke likes singing in the bath.

Luke ______________________ in der Badewanne.

b) It began to rain.

Es ______________________ zu regnen.

c) Sally prefers to do her homework in the kitchen.

Sally ____________ ihre Hausaufgaben ________________ in der Küche.

d) Jane and her friends love dancing to rock music.

Jane und ihre Freundinnen ______________________ zu Rockmusik.

e) Fred doesn't mind walking but he hates running.

Fred hat nichts dagegen zu laufen, aber er ______________________.

f) John was warned, but he continued to interrupt (stören) the lesson.

John wurde ermahnt, aber er ______________________ den Unterricht.

2. **Choose the appropriate continuation for the sentence.**

a) George stopped to make a phone call.

A ☐ The caller wondered what was going on, as George didn't even say goodbye.

B ☐ We waited for him while he used his mobile.

b) Unfortunately we had forgotten to switch the heating off.

A ☐ The house was really warm when we returned from our holiday, and we had wasted a lot of money on heating.

B ☐ We phoned the neighbour we had left the key with. She phoned back to say that we had indeed turned the heating off.

c) Do you remember tidying your room?

A ☐ It took about three hours, it was in such a mess.

B ☐ You really must. An untidy room is unhygienic and not restful to the eye.

d) I had forgotten writing to the estate agents.

A ☐ When the reply came I was rather surprised.

B ☐ Afterwards I realized that we had missed our chance of a good bargain.

e) If you stop thinking …

A ☐ … obviously you're going to make mistakes.

B ☐ … you will realize that conservation of the rainforest is the only way forward.

f) You must remember to write me a postcard.

A ☐ Look, here it is. It arrived yesterday.

B ☐ I'd really like a New Zealand stamp.

22 Stellung der Adverbien

Die wichtigsten Regeln zur Stellung des Adverbs sind folgende:

- Anders als im Deutschen darf das Adverb **nie** zwischen Verb und Objekt stehen (a).
- Im Gegensatz zum Deutschen wird der Ort vor der Zeit genannt (b).

a) Der neue Rektor **spielt** im Verein **Schach**.
*The new headmaster **plays chess** in a club.*

b) Er kommt jeden Tag **um halb acht // in die Schule.**
*He comes **to school // at half past seven** every day.*

1. Underline the adverb / adverbial phrase in each of these sentences. Put a circle around the verb and object.

Example:
Barbara never eats meat.

a) Her mum buys fresh vegetables twice a week.

b) Sometimes Barbara cooks a meal for the whole family.

c) She can make shepherd's pie very well.

d) At the weekend she makes a pizza or spaghetti bolognaise.

e) She often invites her best friend for a meal.

2. Mark (↓) the right place for the adverb in brackets.

Tipp

Häufigkeitsadverbien (z. B. *often*) gehören direkt vor das Hauptverb bzw. unmittelbar hinter das erste Hilfsverb.

a) Ben plays football. (very well)

b) He's playing football. (now)

c) He doesn't play football. (usually; on Saturdays)

d) But there's an important match. (today)

e) He misses a match. (never)

3. Underline the adverbial phrase of place in each sentence.

a) Jo and Dan are going to the cinema this evening.

b) They're going to eat at a fast food place after the film has finished.

c) Dan will bring Jo home at about 11 p.m.

d) Jo's mum goes to bed at ten, so she'll have to be very quiet.

4. Mark (↓) the right position for the phrase or word in brackets in each sentence.

a) Maxi sits until late at night. (at his computer)

b) He surfs for hours. (the Internet)

c) His mum has stopped sending him at night. (to bed)

d) These days, she goes before him. (to bed)

e) In the morning he's supposed to leave at seven thirty. (the house)

f) As you can imagine, he often comes late. (to school)

5. Put the sentence elements into the right order. The Johnsons are going on holiday. Mum is telling Adam how to pack the car.

Das erste Wort bleibt am Anfang.

Tipp

a) Put / in the boot *(Kofferraum)* / first / the big things

b) Then / smaller things / in the spaces / afterwards / put

c) The coats / right on top / when we've finished / go

d) Take / just before we leave / out of the fridge / the sandwiches

23 Modale Hilfsverben

Die englischen Hilfsverben entsprechen nicht immer den deutschen (a).
Die Ersatzformen zu den modalen Hilfsverben *(have to, be allowed to etc.)* sind rein informativ (b).
Die Struktur (Hilfsverb + *have* + *past participle*) funktioniert ähnlich wie im Deutschen, weist aber eine andere Wortstellung auf (c).

a) nicht dürfen ➠ ***mustn't*** ≠ ***nicht müssen*** ➠ *needn't*
b) *Sarah **must** use a wheelchair.* (Ich bestehe darauf.)
*Sarah **has to** use a wheelchair.* (Arme Sarah.)
c) *You needn't have hurried.* Du hättest dich nicht beeilen müssen.

1. **Find a suitable English auxiliary for each German sentence.**

mustn't • needn't • should • can • can't • might

a) Geh nicht bis zum Rand. Du könntest doch hinunterfallen.

b) Mrs. Darke sagt, dass wir erst dann gehen dürfen, wenn wir fertig sind.

c) Gut, also jetzt dürft ihr gehen.

d) Du müsstest die Wörter jeden Tag wiederholen, dann bekommst du eine bessere Note.

e) Du musst nicht auf uns warten. Wir kommen bald nach.

f) Pass gut auf die Kleine auf. Sie darf nicht in der Nähe des Bienenkorbs spielen.

Tipp „erst" heißt im Englischen *not … until*.

2. **Pair up the sentences which belong together with arrows.**

Example:

We mustn't go into the house with our shoes on.	We aren't allowed to go into the house with our shoes on.
It's a house rule.	We might dirty the carpet.

a)

You must walk to school.	You have to walk to school.
There isn't a bus.	You're overweight.

b)

I'm not allowed to waste time.	I mustn't waste any time.
I want to watch the Simpsons.	My mum is very strict about that.

c)

You needn't do the washing up.	You don't have to do the washing up.
You're in a hurry, so I'll do it.	Lucky you!

d)

We shouldn't smoke here.	We aren't supposed to smoke here.
I don't want to upset the non-smokers.	It's a silly rule.

3. Put the words in the right order.

Example:
I've swept the floor for you.
bothered – have – you – needn't.

You needn't have bothered.

a) The dog has escaped! Don't worry,
far – gone – he – have – can't

b) Where's Mum? – I don't know. Look in the kitchen.
a note – us – left – might – she – have

c) Why did you go into the mountains without a map?
easily – lost – could – got – you – have

d) There's a mouse in the kitchen.
by the cat – may – brought in – been – have – it

24 Texte lesen und verstehen

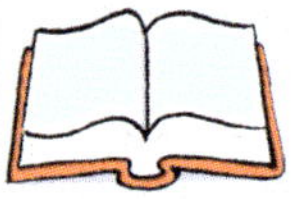

Versuche beim Lesen das Wesentliche aufzunehmen; lass dich von unbekannten Wörtern nicht irritieren. Textverständnis kann z. B. durch *true / false* Aufgaben, *questions on the text* und *text production* überprüft werden. Bei den *questions on the text* sind meistens ganze Sätze verlangt; der Satz muss auch ohne die zugehörige Frage einen Sinn ergeben.

1. Read the text. You don't need to understand everything to complete the task.

The writer has been at a pub in the town and is now on his way home.

> I worked my way drunkenly home, down the path to the river, in the early hours of the morning. It was a hot night, lit only by the stars and, as a reward for not tumbling all of the way down the steep descent, I treated myself to an hour flat on my back on a warm rock in the middle of the river. The nearest street-lighting was far away, so no dull glow marred the perfect blackness of the night sky, and more stars than I had ever seen glowed and winked. I saw literally dozens of shooting stars.
> It must have been the Perseids: mid-August is usually the time for this shower of meteors to pass. But I didn't know about such things then and, anyway, my mind was too occupied with everything I'd heard to think of astronomy. 'It must always be like this on summer nights,' I thought fancifully as I dripped a crooked trail of water up towards the house.

(Driving over Lemons by Chris Stewart, published by Sort Of Books; p. 33)

2. Tick 'right' or 'wrong' for each statement about the text.

		right	wrong
a)	It was a cloudy night.	☐	☐
b)	The time was before midnight.	☐	☐
c)	The writer had never seen so many stars before.	☐	☐
d)	The writer saw at least twenty-four meteors.	☐	☐

e) The writer knew he was seeing the Perseids. ☐ ☐

f) It was the middle of August. ☐ ☐

g) The writer was not thinking about anything particular while he lay on the rock. ☐ ☐

3. **Choose the correct alternative.**

a) At the beginning, the writer is walking

A ☐ along B ☐ towards C ☐ away from the river.

b) The writer lies on a rock because he is

A ☐ angry B ☐ depressed C ☐ pleased with himself.

c) The writer is thinking about

A ☐ a previous conversation B ☐ astronomy C ☐ nothing at all.

4. **Answer the questions on the text in complete sentences. Use the sentence beginnings given.**

What impresses the writer while he is resting on the rock?

The writer is impressed by ______________________________

Which sentence tells you that the writer is not familiar with the area?

We know that ______________________________

____

Why is the trail up to the house 'crooked' (krumm)?

In the first line, we read that the writer ______________________________

____

25 Notizen für einen Text anfertigen

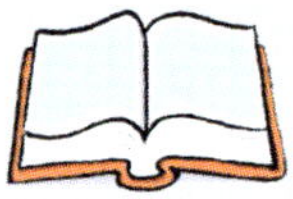

Um ein Referat zu halten oder einen Text über ein bestimmtes Thema zu schreiben, brauchst du Notizen aus zuverlässigen Quellen. Diese Notizen werden dann sinnvoll angeordnet und mit *connecting words* (z. B. Konjunktionen) und Ergänzungen zu einem Text verknüpft.

Hier ist ein Beispiel:
illegal immigrants – no papers – limited job opportunities

Immigrants smuggle themselves over the border because they have no official documents which would allow them to enter the country legally. As a result, they are unlikely to find a job when they arrive.

1. Read the notes and underline the right alternatives.

Hurricane – severe tropical storm – speed > 74 mph (about 120 kmph)
– US coastline Texas / Maine average five hurricanes in three years
– damage: heavy waves; wind

A hurricane is a severe tropical storm with / at a speed of at least 74 miles per hour, or / and around 120 kilometres per hour. In / On average, the US coastline among / between Texas and Maine visits / suffers five hurricanes all / every three years. Damage is caused by / resulted in heavy waves and, however / of course, by the high winds.

2. Read the notes and complete the text with the words given.

Hurricane Andrew – started Africa as minor storm – s. Florida
August 24, 1992 – Category 4 – waves > 17 feet (> 5 metres)
– peak gust 164 mph – too strong for most wind-measuring tools

begun • however • hurricane • Hurricane • in • of • on • or • reached

______________ Andrew hit south Florida ______________ August 24, 1992. It had ______________ as a minor tropical storm ______________ Africa. By the time it ______________ south Florida it had become a Category 4 ______________, causing waves of over 17 feet ______________ 5 metres. A peak gust ______________ 164 mph (262 kmph) was recorded. ______________, the wind was too strong for most wind-measuring tools.

3. **Use these notes to continue the text. Then compare your text with the model solution at the back of the book. You can change words, e.g. death ➠ died**

23 deaths US + 3 Bahamas – $26.5 billion damage, mostly s. Florida – since 1992 improvement of measuring equipment and early warning systems – better preparation

____

____

____

____

____

____

____

____

____

26 Informationen sinnvoll anordnen

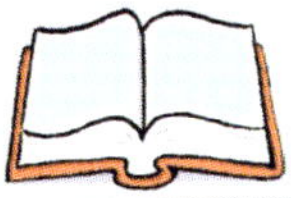

Notizen für ein Referat können aus verschiedenen Quellen stammen und müssen sinnvoll kombiniert werden.

Diese Notizen aus zwei Quellen beziehen sich auf Weihnachten in den USA.
Christmas Eve – shops open late
Christmas Eve – buy last minute presents
In einem Text könnten sie so zusammengeführt werden:
In America the shops are open late on Christmas Eve so that people can buy some last minute presents.

1. Underline the information about food in the three sets of notes.

a) Christmas Eve: preparation of food, last minute shopping, stockings hung up, no special meal.
Christmas Day: presents opened round tree, big meal, lazy afternoon, lots of sweets.

b) Christmas Eve: shops open late, food bought, perhaps midnight mass, Santa Claus / chimney.
Christmas Day: children unpack stockings (traditionally fruit and nuts, nowadays chocolate and other presents), no shops open, church in the morning, turkey and Christmas pudding, paper hats and crackers.

c) Advent: advent calendar, often with a sweet for each day; no special church events.
Christmas Eve: increasing excitement, everyone busy with last-minute preparations; shops very busy, especially sale of turkeys.
Christmas Day: children up at dawn to open stockings – probably eating sweets from stocking before breakfast; mothers spend morning in the kitchen preparing meal; turkey with vegetables and sauces, wine, followed by Christmas pudding. Afternoon walk or watching TV.

2. You are giving a talk with two others about Christmas in America. Your topic is food. Combine the underlined parts above to make a coherent text.

In America food plays a very important role in the Christmas festivities. It starts at the beginning of December, as most advent calendars ______________________________

There is no ______________________________ *on Christmas Eve, but* ______________________________

____

____

On Christmas Day the eating starts before ______________________________

____

____

Traditionally, the stockings ______________________________

____

The big meal of the day ______________________________

____

____

After dinner, ______________________________

____

27 Textproduktion

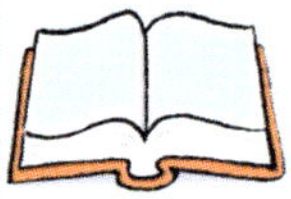

Einem Lesetext wird häufig eine Aufgabe zur *text production* angehängt. Der Text wird als Ausgangspunkt für einen Brief, Bericht oder Ähnliches verwendet. Hier handelt es sich um einen Brief. Gehe so vor:

1. Markiere die Textteile, die du brauchst.
2. Mache knappe Notizen, achte darauf, dass du den Text nicht abschreibst.
3. Füge einen Vorspann und Schlussteil an. Hier kannst du deine Fantasie walten lassen.

1. Read the text from 'The Lion, the Witch and the Wardrobe' by C.S. Lewis.

It is summer, and Lucy is staying at a large house in the country with her sister and two brothers. She has just stepped into a wardrobe[1] and met a faun[2] called Tumnus, in a strange winter landscape[3].

"Allow me to introduce myself. My name is Tumnus."
"I am very pleased to meet you, Mr Tumnus," said Lucy.
"And may I ask, O Lucy Daughter of Eve," said Mr Tumnus, "how you have come into Narnia?"
"Narnia? What's that?"
"This is the land of Narnia," said the Faun, "where we are now; all that lies between the lamp-post[4] and the great castle of Cair Paravel on the eastern sea. And you – you have come from the wild woods of the west?"
"I – I got in through the wardrobe in the spare room[5]," said Lucy.
"Ah!" said Mr Tumnus in a rather melancholy voice, "if only I had worked harder at geography when I was a little Faun, I should no doubt know all about those strange countries. It is too late now."
"But they aren't countries at all," said Lucy, almost laughing. "It's only just back there – at least – I'm not sure. It is summer there."
"Meanwhile", said Mr Tumnus, " it is winter in Narnia, and has been for ever so long, and we shall both catch cold if we stand here talking in the snow. Daughter of Eve from the far land of Spare Oom where eternal[6] summer reigns around the bright city of War Drobe, how would it be if you came and had tea with me?"

(The Lion, the Witch and the Wardrobe by C.S. Lewis, published by Collins London)

1 ***wardrobe*** – Kleiderschrank; 2 ***faun*** – Faun (lüsterner Mensch); 3 ***landscape*** – Landschaft; 4 ***lamp-post*** – Lampenstiel; 5 ***spare room*** – Gästezimmer; 6 ***eternal*** – ewig

2. The story is written from Lucy's point of view. Imagine you are the faun. Write a letter to a friend about the meeting with Lucy. Don't forget the introduction and a suitable ending.

28 Wortfeld: Geschichte Amerikas

Einige Begriffe werden nur oder überwiegend in Bezug auf Amerika benutzt. Das betrifft insbesondere Wörter, die mit der Einwanderung und mit den Besonderheiten der Geschichte der USA zu tun haben.

ancestor – Vorfahre
persecution – Verfolgung
liberty – Freiheit
slavery – Sklaverei
plantation – Plantage
declaration – Erklärung

1. In each group there is one word which doesn't fit. Underline the odd word out.

a) settlers – Inuit – Hispanic – immigrant

b) Declaration of Independence – colony – silicon valley – gold rush

c) prairie – downtown – skyscraper – shopping mall

2. Try to complete the crossword.

Across

3. People in your family who lived before you.
4. The state of being poor.
5. The search for gold in the 1840s. (Two words.)
8. A very large area of grassland (usually without any trees) in N. America.
10. Being bullied (persecuted) because of religious or political beliefs.
11. Native Americans who live in Alaska.
12. Large fields with sugar plants, where slaves from Africa had to work.
13. Anyone who came from another country to live in America.

Down

1. A political group which rules (governs) a country or state.
2. The document signed on July 4th 1776, which stated that the USA no longer belonged to Britain, was called the … of Independence.
6. Immigrants were welcomed by a monument which promised freedom. Another word for freedom.
7. A place where Native Americans can live and keep their culture alive.
9. A new town where settlers lived.

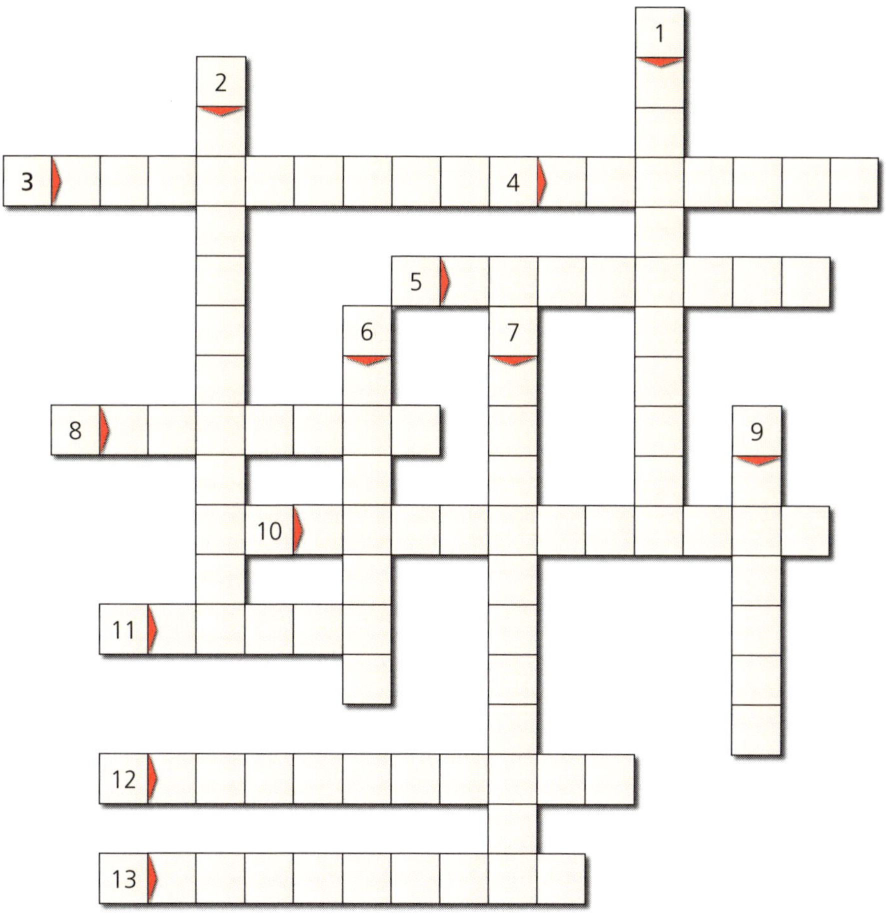

29 Amerikanisches und britisches Englisch

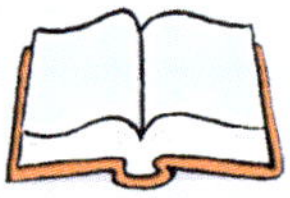

Amerikaner und Briten können sich problemlos miteinander verständigen. Trotzdem gibt es in beiden Sprachen unterschiedliche Wörter für die gleiche Sache.

BE	AE
shop	store
lift	elevator
autumn	fall

1. Find the most sensible alternative for each sentence in American English.

Example: You can either use the elevator or walk up. / go jogging.

a) In the fall Steve will break his leg. / be in the tenth grade.

b) In winter it's useful to have a sled instead of a baby buggy. / tent.

c) I hope your vacation doesn't hurt! / is fun!

d) It's nice to spend an evening at the movie theater so that you can get some exercise. / relax and forget about real life for a while.

e) The exhibition goes on from 2nd September through the streets. / 4th October.

2. Kristin is American. She's staying with old Mrs Barton, a British lady who never watches American films or reads American books. Help them with their misunderstandings.

Example:

Kristin: It's neat here.

Mrs Barton: Yes, it is tidy, isn't it?

You: *She means it's very nice here.*

a) Kristin: At my school the students don't wear uniform.

Mrs Barton: No, I don't suppose they do. But the children do, don't they?

You: No, no, Mrs Barton. She means that ______________________

______________________ wear uniform.

b) Mrs Barton: The bathroom is first on the right.

Kristin: Oh – but there's only a bathtub and a shower in there.

Mrs Barton: Well, what more do you want?

You: Sorry, Mrs Barton, but she really wants ______________________

____

c) Mrs Barton: Your room is upstairs.

Kristin: Oh, right, on the second floor.

Mrs Barton: I haven't got a second floor, young lady.

You: Kristin, in Britain they say second floor when they mean

____

d) Kristin: My second name begins with zee, so I'm always the last on lists of names.

Mrs Barton: Did you say cee? That's near the beginning of the alphabet.

You: No, Mrs Barton, she said zee.

That's ____

30 Besonderheiten der Rechtschreibung im amerikanischen Englisch

Die Rechtschreibregeln im amerikanischen Englisch unterscheiden sich teilweise von denen im britischen Englisch.

AE: *hon**or**; cent**er**; trave**l**ing; progra**m***
BE: *hon**our**; cent**re**; trave**ll**ing; progra**mme**.*

Beide Schreibweisen sind akzeptabel,
sollten in einem Text aber nicht gemischt werden:
The theater is in the center of the town.
~~*The theater is in the centre of the town.*~~

My favourite restaurant is near the harbour.
~~*My favorite restaurant is near the harbour.*~~

1. **Identify the following sentences as AE (American English) or BE (British English).**

a) Eliza does lots of different sports, but her favourite is swimming.

☐ AE ☐ BE

b) An inch is about two point four centimetres.

☐ AE ☐ BE

c) Red is a rather aggressive color.

☐ AE ☐ BE

d) A special church service is held in November to honor the dead from the two World Wars.

☐ AE ☐ BE

e) The pioneers traveled west, looking for new territory.

☐ AE ☐ BE

2. **Choose the right alternative so that you don't mix American and British English.**

Example:
If you ask little girls what their favorite colour / <u>color</u> is, most of them will say pink.

a) There was a programme about acting and the theater / theatre generally.

b) The harbour isn't far from the town centre / center.

c) During the gold rush people traveled thousands of kilometres / kilometers, hoping to get rich the easy way.

3. **Find the American spelling in each group.**

a) honor – programme – travelled

b) centre – favourite – meters

c) colour – centimetre – harbor

d) theatre – traveling – honour

31 Übersetzungsmöglichkeiten für „vor"

Das deutsche Wort „vor" hat vier gängige Übersetzungen im Englischen: *before, in front of, ago, to.*

vor + Ort	*There's a garden* ***in front of*** *the house.*
vor + Zeitpunkt / Ereignis	*Don't eat chocolate* ***before*** *dinner.*
vor + Zeitraum	*Laura passed her driving test six weeks* ***ago.***
vor bei Uhrzeiten	*Hurry up! It's ten* ***to*** *nine.*

Nicht verwechseln:

vor sechs Wochen	*six weeks* ***ago***
sechs Wochen ***lang***	***for*** *six weeks*

1. **Underline possible context words. There may be more than one!**

a) in front of the house / eight / the lesson / the class

b) in front of next week / the camera / the teacher / evening

c) before the concert / the school / a week / the end of term

d) before winter / sunset / a few years / the computer

2. **Underline the right word for the context. Only one is correct.**

a) Adam started learning judo two months ago / before.

b) The instruction begins at quarter to / before eight every Thursday.

c) The instructor stands in front of / before the students.

d) The students have to greet him properly in front of / before the lesson starts.

3. **Translate into German.**

a) Quentin's sister went to America two years ago.

____

b) Quentin stayed with his sister in New York for two months.

____

4. **Find the right context for each sentence.**

a) A ☐ How long did you learn Spanish?

B ☐ When did you learn Spanish?

– Two years ago.

b) We lived in France for ten years. –

A ☐ During the twelve months that we were there, my French improved dramatically.

B ☐ I was only eight when we went there, and just before we left I passed my driving test.

c) It rained for two days. –

A ☐ The river overflowed its banks.

B ☐ It wasn't enough to really wet the earth.

32 „Gern", „hoffentlich" etc. auf Englisch

Bestimmte deutsche Adverbien werden im Englischen mit einem Verb ausgedrückt.

gern – *like (doing)*
lieber – *prefer (doing)*
bestimmt – *I'm sure*
hoffentlich – *I hope*
vermutlich – *I expect*
anscheinend – *seem*

1. **Match the English and German sentences.**

Jetzt ist Tony bestimmt zu Hause.		Tony seems to be at home.
Vermutlich ist Tony jetzt zu Hause.		I hope Tony is at home.
Tony ist anscheinend zu Hause.		I'm sure Tony is at home.
Hoffentlich ist Tony zu Hause.		I expect Tony is at home.

2. **Translate into German. Use the words given.**

hoffentlich • vermutlich • gern • anscheinend • lieber • bestimmt

On a climbing trip …

a) I like climbing.

b) I hope the weather will stay nice.

c) You seem to be frightened.

d) I'm sure you won't fall.

e) Would you prefer to watch me climbing?

3. Frau Weber is renting a holiday cottage out to an English family. She has left them a note on the kitchen table. Translate the *italic* parts into English.

Liebe Familie Thornton,

willkommen im Allgäu! *Hoffentlich hatten Sie eine angenehme Reise.*

a) ______________________________

Ich habe Milch und Brot für Sie eingekauft – *Sie haben nach Ihrer Reise bestimmt Hunger.* b) ______________________________

____

Wenn Sie gerne wandern (walking) c) ______________________________

____

können Sie zur Schlossanger Alp hinaufsteigen. *Aber vielleicht schwimmen Sie lieber.* d) ______________________________

____

In Pfronten gibt es ein schönes Hallenbad. Früher hatte das Hallenbad montags zu, *jetzt ist es anscheinend jeden Tag offen.*

e) ______________________________

____

Das Wetter ist zu dieser Jahreszeit meistens sehr schön, *also werden Sie vermutlich viel Sonne haben.* f) ______________________________

____

Eine schöne Zeit wünscht

Elfriede Weber

33 Übersetzungstraining

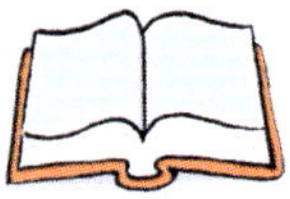

Beim Übersetzen sollte man den Inhalt so genau wie möglich wiedergeben, gleichzeitig aber gutes, flüssiges Deutsch schreiben. Das heißt, dass man den Mut haben muss, eine Struktur notfalls frei wiederzugeben.

*This statement must sound **like a sick joke** to a large number of children in the world, and that is what this article is all about.*
Dass für einen großen Teil der Kinder auf der Welt diese Aussage **wie Hohn** klingen muss, davon handelt dieser Artikel.

1. Translate the sentences, using the vocabulary given.

a) It's worth finding out about cheap flights.
sich informieren / sich lohnen

____

b) Big blocks of flats are not very suitable for children.
Hochhaus / kinderfreundlich

____

c) Most people don't mind litter.
sich stören lassen / Abfälle

____

d) You have to wear a helmet.
Pflicht

____

e) David is at university at the moment.
Studium

____

f) The boys made a big effort and they succeeded in reaching the top of the mountain.
sich anstrengen / gelingen / Gipfel

____

g) Ramona isn't going to eat any chocolate during Lent.
vorhaben / Fastenzeit / verzichten

2. **Translate the following passage. Decide which of the alternatives in brackets to use.**

When (wenn / als) I left my family I imagined everything was easy. There were six of us children (wir waren / es gab) at home, my mother didn't have (hatte nicht / hatte keine) a proper job and we hadn't seen my father for (für / seit) weeks. Before I left the hut, I told my mother that I was going to (ich wollte / ich ging) look for work. After all (nach alledem / schließlich), I was the eldest son. But it's difficult to find work when you're (man / du) only (erst / nur) eleven.

34 „Falsche Freunde" – Textverständnis

Ein ***false friend*** ist ein englisches Wort, das einem deutschen ähnlich sieht, aber eine andere Bedeutung hat.

hall	⇐	Flur	≠	*floor*	⇒	Boden
bouquet	⇐	Bukett	≠	*bucket*	⇒	Eimer
give, donate	⇐	spenden	≠	*spend*	⇒	ausgeben

1. Find the right translation from the box and write it in the space.

blamieren, Fußboden, Mappe, bestehen, beschuldigen, tapfer, streng, brav, Landkarte, verpassen, stark, Flur

a) floor ____________

b) map ____________

c) pass ____________

d) strong ____________

e) blame ____________

f) brave ____________

2. **Choose the right context.**

a) The girls go to the gymnasium.
A ☐ They hope to pass the A-levels.
B ☐ They hope to get fit.

b) The teacher gave us a note.
A ☐ I got a four and my friend got a three.
B ☐ We took it to the school office.

c) Take your map with you.
A ☐ Otherwise you might get lost.
B ☐ Then you'll have all your papers with you.

d) I might pass the exam.
A ☐ Then I can go to university.
B ☐ Then I'll have to take it again.

e) The football fans were very noisy, so the police had to control them.
A ☐ They checked their pockets.
B ☐ They made them walk quietly.

f) To be a good nurse, you have to be patient.
A ☐ Then you know what it's like to be in a hospital bed.
B ☐ Sometimes the work is frustrating, but you have to keep calm.

g) Mrs Brown's son is going to high school next year.
A ☐ He's eleven.
B ☐ He's eighteen.

h) Mrs Benton is strong.
A ☐ If you haven't got your homework she gives you fifty lines to write.
B ☐ She can carry the overhead projector.

35 „Falsche Freunde“ – Textproduktion

Es passiert ganz leicht, dass man ein vermeintlich bekanntes englisches Wort in einem falschen Zusammenhang verwendet.

*I've bought two **cards** for the concert.* ➠ *tickets*
*Schumacher **spent** ten million euros for the victims of the flood.* ➠ *gave*

1. Underline the right word.

a) The police found a murder / a murderer who had escaped from prison.

b) A gorilla is a kind / an art of ape.

c) Call Ann. If she's not at home, try her mobile / handy number.

d) Waiter, could we have the card, / menu, please?

e) In the old days, people had servants. They just rang the clock / bell and a servant appeared.

2. Underline the mistake in each sentence and correct it using one of these words. You don't need all the words.

work · good · ~~boss~~ · makes · make a fool of · give · hutch · horse

a) Fiona has got a new job. She likes the work, but her ~~chief~~ boss isn't very friendly.

b) The neighbours have got a rabbit stall in their garden.

c) I'd like to try playing the trumpet, but I don't want to blame myself.

d) Johnny always does what he's told. He's such a brave boy.

e) Dave's dad has won a computer in a competition. He's going to spend it to the school.

3. **Complete the translations using some of the words from the box.**

art mobiles kind chips
note mark crisps
notices handy notes

a) Für Notfälle sind Handys sehr praktisch.

_______________ are very useful for emergencies.

b) Für eine Party kauft man am besten Chips und Cola.

_______________ and cola are the best things to buy for a party.

c) Der Amsel ist eine Art Singvogel.

The blackbird is a _______________ of songbird.

d) Die Schüler machten Notizen.

The students made _______________.

e) Wenn du mehr schreibst, bekommst du nicht unbedingt eine bessere Note.

You don't necessarily get a better _______________ if you write more.

36 Wörter im richtigen Zusammenhang verwenden

Wenn ein deutsches Wort zwei oder mehr Übersetzungen hat, muss man die richtige für den jeweiligen Zusammenhang wählen.

While Anne was at the disco her ***bag*** */* ~~***pocket***~~ *was stolen.*

1. Which German word fits both meanings?

a) heavy — difficult — ____________

b) pillow — cushion — ____________

c) throat — neck — ____________

d) remind — remember — ____________

e) another — a different — ____________

f) price — prize — ____________

g) ready — finished — ____________

h) lesson — hour — ____________

i) pocket — bag — ____________

2. **Give the right English word for the German word in brackets.**

a) When George arrived he was carrying a big ______ over his shoulder. (Tasche)

b) He had won a ______ at the fairground. (Preis)

c) The students are allowed to draw a picture on the back of the test paper when they ______. (fertig sind)

d) There are five maths ______ a week. (Stunden)

e) ______ me to switch the oven off before we go out. (erinnern)

f) One of the first signs of a cold is a sore ______. It hurts to swallow. (Hals)

g) Some people go to sleep as soon as their head touches the ______. (Kopfkissen)

h) The exam was very ______. Most of the students think they've failed it. (schwer)

i) I'd like to buy this pullover, but there's a fault in it. – Oh, I'll find you ______ one in exactly the same design and colour. (einen anderen)

37 Feste Wendungen im Englischen

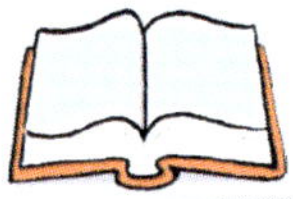

Genauso wie im Deutschen gibt es im Englischen feste Wendungen mit zwei oder mehr Wörtern.

instead of – statt

to get lost – sich verlaufen

everyday life – der Alltag

1. **Translate the underlined parts into German.**

a) Suddenly out of the blue we had a phone call from Dora.

____ (three words)

b) We had heard nothing from her for years, except for Christmas cards.

____ (one word)

c) She lives a long way away, in Scotland.

____ (one word)

d) We can't help her much, of course.

____ (one word)

e) She will have to do it on her own.

____ (one word)

2. **Underline the right alternative.**

a) Can you give me a / some / any hand with this cupboard?

b) The new flat felt strange at first, but we got used at / with / to it.

c) There's one advantage: we're close near / to / at the shops.

d) Gwen's dad is often away in / on / with business.

e) He's away on / for / at least twice a month.

f) I'm not going to buy a season ticket. It's not worth to / it / itself.

3. Find a word from the box to go in each gap. There are some extra words which you won't need.

says	thank	does	for	stores	
shops	goes	little	matter	in	
at	in	short	left		

a) Kevin is interested ________ model cars.

b) Clara is out of hospital again, ________ goodness.

c) Sarah loves horses. She ________ riding every weekend.

d) In the city centre there are department ________ where you can buy practically anything.

e) You look terrible. What's the ________?

f) Where's your homework? – I'm sorry, but I ________ it at home.

g) We can go the long way round, or we can take a ________ cut through the park.

h) It ________ in the newspaper that it's going to rain tomorrow.

i) We weren't sure what to do, but ________ the end we decided to stay at home.

38 Phrasal verbs

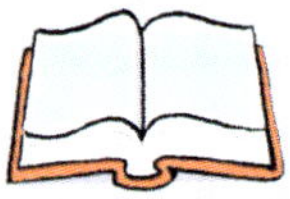

Eine feste Einheit, die aus Verb plus Partikel besteht, ist ein ***phrasal verb.*** Im *phrasal verb* ist die Bedeutung des Verbs häufig etwas verändert.

Bei *to look forward to* (sich freuen auf) heißt *look* nicht „schauen"; *bei to pick up* (aufheben, abholen) heißt *pick* nicht „pflücken". Beachte das Gerund nach *to look forward to*:
*I'm looking forward to **seeing** you in July / **meeting** Julie.*

1. Translate the following sentences into German.

a) Are you looking forward to the party?

____

b) If you don't know a word you can look it up in the dictionary.

____

c) Darren's walking on his hands, but ignore him. He's just showing off.

____

d) Here are the paints. Pick out the colours you need.

____

e) I want to be a nurse, but I don't know what exams I need to pass.
– Well, find out, then.

____

____

2. Underline the right alternative.

a) Can I speak to Mrs Green, please? –
Yes, certainly, I'll put you in / through / on.

b) Can I speak to Gerry, please? – OK, I'll get him. Just hang on / in / up a moment.

c) After the party Victoria's mum is picking us out / up / from and taking us home.

d) Climbing the mountain was more difficult than Roger had expected, but he didn't give up / over / on. He made it in the end.

e) The theatre group are putting up / over / on a Shakespeare play at the end of term.

3. **Add the correct particle from the box. There is one extra word.**

after • around • down • for • forward • out

a) We are looking ________ to our holiday.

b) An au pair does housework and looks ________ the children.

c) There's a mouse in the kitchen but we can't work ________ how it got in.

d) In the holidays Geoff doesn't know what to do with himself. He just hangs ________ at home.

e) Tom has hurt his knee. He fell ________ at the playground this morning.

4. **Add a suitable verb in the -ing form in each sentence.**

a) We're looking forward to ________ you at Easter.

b) Jo is looking forward to ________ to her new CD.

c) Grandad is looking forward to ________ the book of the film.

d) Ben is looking forward to ________ to France.

e) And you? What are you looking forward to?

____

39 Mengen- und Zeitangaben in Aussagesätzen und Fragen/Verneinungen

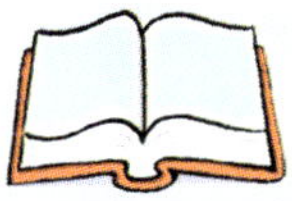

Gelegentlich muss man unterschiedliche Ausdrücke für Mengen- und Zeitangaben oder für Entfernungen nehmen, je nachdem, ob es sich um einen Aussagesatz oder um eine Frage / Verneinung handelt. Die Ausdrücke in der linken Spalte sollten auf keinen Fall in Aussagesätzen verwendet werden, während in der gesprochenen Sprache ein Ausdruck aus der rechten Spalte in einer Frage oder Verneinung möglich ist.

Frage / Verneinung	Aussagesatz
far	*a long way*
long	*a long time*
much / many	*a lot*

1. Fill in a long time / a long way / a lot / a lot of.

a) The youth club is ________________ away, but it isn't far from here to the swimming pool.

b) Have you been waiting long? – Yes, I've been waiting for ________________ – about half an hour. Where have you been?

c) Is it far to the nearest post office? – Yes, I'm afraid it's quite ________________ to walk.

d) How many people have you invited to the party? – Oh, quite ________________ – about twenty.

e) Hans has lived in England for ________________. He's been there since the war.

f) ________________ children have signed up for the art club, so they're making two groups.

2. **Fill in** a long time / long. **The style is formal, written English.**

a) The first speakers of English arrived in Britain ____________________ ago from North Germany.

b) It didn't take them ____________________ to frighten the Celts away.

c) They stayed in the east of the country for ____________________, but they gradually spread westwards.

d) But although the Celts were forced into the corners of Britain, their language has survived for ____________________.

3. **Fill in** a long way / far. **The style is formal, written English.**

a) Nowadays with modern ferries, south-east England does not seem to be ____________________ from the north of Germany.

b) But in the fifth century A.D. it was ____________________ for the primitive little boats which the Angles and Saxons travelled in.

c) It was ____________________ back again, too, so most of them stayed and colonized Britain.

4. **Fill in** much / a lot of. **The style is formal, written English.**

a) When the Angles and Saxons arrived in Britain they found ____________________ good farming land.

b) They had ____________________ experience in farming.

c) The Celts did not have ____________________ luck.

d) There was ____________________ fighting but eventually the Celts had to give up.

40 Unregelmäßige Verben I: simple past

Hier wird das ***simple past*** unregelmäßiger Verben geübt.

speak	➠	*spoke*	*hurt*	➠	*hurt*
ring	➠	*rang*	*fly*	➠	*flew*

1. Write down the infinitive of these simple past forms.

a) felt ____________________ *b)* drove ____________________

c) ate ____________________ *d)* read ____________________

e) fell ____________________ *f)* wore ____________________

g) slept ____________________

2. Write down the simple past form of these infinitives.

a) choose ____________________ *b)* sell ____________________

c) write ____________________ *d)* go ____________________

e) take ____________________ *f)* spend ____________________

g) understand ____________________

3. Add the simple past or the infinitive of the verb in brackets.

a) Catherine ______________ well in the race. (run)

b) But she didn't __________________ the race. (win)

c) She ____________________. (lose)

d) Another girl _______________ to the winning post before her. (get)

e) Did Catherine ___________________ in the pool afterwards? (swim)

f) No, she didn't. She ____________________ straight home. (go)

4. Highlight the simple past forms. There are eleven of them.

told	caught	saw	meet	give
drove	break	lend	shone	were
meant	bent	made	come	lie
knew	phone	lead	build	held

5. Find the odd one out. The simple past form of one verb in each group doesn't rhyme with the simple past forms of the other two.

Example:
pay – lie – make ➠ paid – lay – made; the odd one out is 'lie'.

a) ring, bring, think

b) sell, tell, feel

c) show, know, throw

d) cast, cost, lose

e) buy, catch, draw

f) say, feed, shut

41 Unregelmäßige Verben II: past participle

Beim *present perfect (they have begun), past perfect (they had drawn)* und beim Passiv in allen Zeitformen *(it was chosen, the bell is rung)* braucht man das ***past participle,*** die dritte Form des Verbs. Meistens ist sie mit der *simple past* Form identisch, bei einigen wenigen unregelmäßigen Verben aber nicht.

	simple past	*past participle*
write	*wrote*	*written*
know	*knew*	*known*
wake	*woke*	*woken*

1. Highlight the verbs whose past participle is different from the simple past form. There are seven of them.

shake · find · hold · ride · make · tell · have · drink · come · shoot · feed · think · grow · stand · keep · go · eat · let · sit · send

2. Give the infinitive of these past participles.

a) felt ____________ *b)* fallen ____________

c) gone ____________ *d)* worn ____________

e) spoken ____________

3. **Give the past participle of these infinitives.**

a) be ______________________ b) choose ______________________

c) ride ______________________ d) do ______________________

e) hide ______________________

4. **Add the simple past and the past participle of the verb in brackets.**

a) Terry and his sister ____________ their homework in the kitchen yesterday.
It was all ______________ by nine o'clock. (do)

b) Who's ______________ all the lemonade? – I have.
I ______________ it because I was thirsty. (drink)

c) Yesterday evening Susan ________________ to her godmother on the phone. She hadn't ________________ to her for several months. (speak)

5. **Add the past participle of a suitable verb from the box.
There is one extra verb, which you don't need.**

be catch forget see become draw show

a) I'm sorry, but I've ____________________ your name.

b) This picture was ____________________ by a boy of nine.

c) The criminal was ____________________ by several people over a few days.

d) Eventually, the thief was ____________________ by the police.

e) Have I ________________ you the wedding photos?

f) Have you ever ____________________ to America?

42 Unregelmäßige Pluralformen

Beachte, dass Nomen ohne eine Pluralendung im Deutschen (Poster, Farmer, Euro) im Englischen den Plural ganz normal mit -s bilden *(posters, farmers, euros)*.
Bei Wendungen, wie *an eight-hour day, a two-man band,* wird das Bezugsnomen im Singular verwendet.

Unregelmäßige Pluralformen sind z. B.
person – people, goose – geese, fish – fish, shelf – shelves.

1. Give the singular form of these plurals.

a) yourselves ____________ *b)* wives ____________

c) knives ____________ *d)* settlers ____________

e) litres ____________

2. Give the singular form of these plurals.

a) geese ____________ *b)* deer ____________

c) women ____________ *d)* people ____________

e) feet ____________

3. **Give the plural form.**

a) life ______________________ *b)* knife ______________________

c) scarf ______________________ *d)* thief ______________________

e) computer ______________________ *f)* monster ______________________

g) euro ______________________ *h)* kilometre ______________________

i) winter ______________________

4. **Give the plural form.**

a) man ______________________ *b)* child ______________________

c) tooth ______________________ *d)* sheep ______________________

e) mouse ______________________ *f)* fish ______________________

5. **Complete the phrases with the words given.**

a) a two-____________ bag of sugar

b) the eight-____________ flight to the USA

c) a twenty-____________ walk

d) a ten-____________ document

e) a two-____________ bottle

f) a four-____________ word

hour
letter
litre
minute
page
pound

43 Wortfeld: Schule in den USA

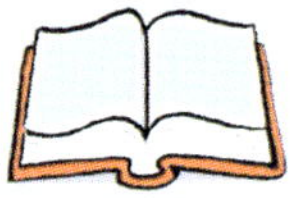

Als sich Siedler von den Britischen Inseln in Amerika niederließen, gab es noch keinen festen Wortschatz zum Thema Schule. So entwickelte sich in den USA ein eigener Wortschatz dazu, der vom britischen Englisch stark abweicht.

Viele amerikanische „Schulwörter“ gehören in Großbritannien zur Universität: *campus, principal, vacation, student, diploma, graduate.*

Das Wort *high school* erinnert an das deutsche „Hochschule“, bezeichnet aber eine Schule für Dreizehn- bis Achtzehnjährige.

Das Wort *students* für „Schüler“ hat auch in Großbritannien Einzug gehalten.

1. 'Call my bluff'. In this game you have to decide which is the right definition or synonym. Underline the correct one.

a)	campus:	school camp	school grounds
b)	principal:	head of a school	school rule
c)	notebook:	exercise book	portable computer
d)	vacation:	job	holiday
e)	cheerleader:	class representative	team representative
f)	schedule:	school timetable	small building for equipment
g)	soccer:	a game with a ball	a sports teacher

2. Match the American nouns to the explanations.

classes • diploma • football • grade •
period • student council • yearbook

a) the school year that a particular student is in: ____________________

b) a rough game where the players wear helmets: ____________________

c) a lesson: ____________________

d) lessons: ______________________________

e) a group of children who make decisions: ______________________________

f) a report about school life over the past year: ______________________________

g) final qualification on leaving high school: ______________________________

3. **Annika has problems with American English. Complete the translation.**

Hi Annika, I'm real glad that you're going to be my pen pal. I guess you'd like to know something about my school. Well, since classes started again after the vacation I've been in tenth grade. In two years' time I'm going to graduate. In our schedule we have six periods of fifty-four minutes each. My favorite subject is Math. The best thing about school is football. I also play soccer and baseball. What about you?
Write soon,
Greg

Hallo Annika!

Ich bin echt froh, dass du meine ______________________________ wirst.

Bestimmt möchtest du etwas über meine Schule erfahren. Also, seitdem

______________________________ nach ______________________________ wieder

angefangen hat, bin ich ______________________________.

In zwei Jahren werde ich ______________________________.

In unserem ______________________________ haben wir sechs

______________________________ von je vierundfünfzig Minuten.

Mein Lieblingsfach ist ______________________________.

Das Beste an der Schule ist ______________________________.

Ich spiele auch ______________________________.

Test 1 – Kapitel 1 bis 5, 12

Wiederholung Zeitformen – simple und progressive, will-future und going to-future, past perfect

1. **Underline the right alternative.**

a) When you phoned I had / was having a shower, so I couldn't come to the phone. We have got / are having a new shower in the bathroom. It's great.

b) Phil is living in France at the moment. He thinks / is thinking that France is a nice place, and he likes the family he's staying with. He's very quiet at the moment, but he doesn't think / isn't thinking about home, he's busy with his homework.

___ / 4

2. **Put the verb into the past simple or progressive.**

"I ________ (try) to phone you yesterday but nobody ________ (pick up) the phone. It was about five o'clock. What ________ (you / do) at that time? Can you remember?"

"Yes, sure. I ________ (play) football at the park. I ________ (go) home at six."

___ / 5

3. **Choose the right context sentence.**

a) I've decorated the living room for the party tonight.
A ☐ Doesn't it look nice? B ☐ My arms are hurting.

b) Has Kevin been doing his homework?
A ☐ It's nearly bedtime. B ☐ There are books all over the table.

c) Tess has been going to bed late recently.
A ☐ And is she still asleep?
B ☐ Oh, did she go to lots of parties last week?

d) Mum has phoned Auntie Mabel.
A ☐ Auntie Mabel says we can stay with her in the summer holidays.
B ☐ Mum has got a headache.

e) We've been looking at the photos of our holiday in Greece.
A ☐ We've decided which ones we want to keep.
B ☐ I wish we were still there!

___ / 5

4. **Complete the sentences with will or is / are going to.**

a) Look at those clouds. It ______ rain.

b) I hope the weather ______ be nice tomorrow.

c) Kevin and I ______ have a picnic by the river tomorrow.

d) We ______ take our swimming trunks with us, of course.

e) Kevin's mum ______ buy some cheese and salad for us.

f) I expect she ______ make sandwiches as usual. ___ / 6

5. **Underline the correct alternative.**

a) Oh, look! Mum made / has made a chocolate cake.
b) But the cat already ate / has already eaten part of the cream on top.
c) Do you remember the time when the cat stole / has stolen the cheese?
d) And once she climbed / has climbed up the apple tree. We had to rescue her.
e) She was only a kitten then. She never did / has never done anything so bad since then. ___ / 5

6. **Put the verb into the correct form: past perfect (had done) or past progressive (was doing).**

When the lights went out …

a) Tom ______ (not finish) cleaning his teeth in the bathroom.

b) Mum ______ (wash) the dishes. She had to finish them in the dark.

c) Alice ______ (write) an e-mail. She checked it for spelling mistakes, but she couldn't send it because the computer went off.

d) Felix was already in bed. He ______ (read) a book, and couldn't finish the chapter. ___ / 5

e) Dad wasn't at home. He ______ (go) to the chess club. ___ / 30

Test 2 – Kapitel 6 bis 9, 15 bis 17, 22

Aktiv und Passiv, indirekte Rede, Stellung der Adverbien

1. **Choose the right alternative.**

a) These keys found / were found at the playground this afternoon.
b) The end-of-term reports write / are written by the teachers.
c) The Smiths always eat / are always eaten together in the evening.
d) The cat brought / was brought a mouse into the kitchen yesterday.
e) If a bee stings you, it hurts / is hurt.

___ / 5

2. **Put these passive sentences into the right order.**

a) the twins / been / by / new mobile phones / their uncle / given / have

____

b) slept / been / in / this bed / already / has

____

c) are / by / after / the children / a neighbour / looked / every day

____

d) tea with milk / were / we / offered

____

e) shown / the house / by / the visitors / were / a servant / round

____

___ / 5

3. **Complete the reported speech.**

a) Philip: I'm going to sleep at the new house tonight.

Sarah: Philip says that ________ ________ going to sleep at the new house tonight.

b) Sarah: I want to sleep late on Sunday.

Philip: Don't phone Sarah before eleven. She says ______ ______ to sleep late on Sunday.

c) Philip: My bedroom is cold. Yours is warmer, Sarah.

Sarah: Philip says ______ bedroom is cold.

He says ______ is warmer.

d) Sarah: I can't find my watch.

Philip: Sarah says ______ can't find ______ watch.

e) Sarah: I haven't seen your new mobile.

Philip: Sarah says ______ ______ seen ______ new mobile.

/ 5

4. **Complete the reported speech in the past.**

a) I'm watching the Simpsons at the moment. – Philip phoned from the new house last night. He said he ______ the Simpsons at the time.

b) I've put up most of the kitchen cupboards. – He told me he ______ up most of the kitchen cupboards.

c) The neighbours invited me in for coffee this morning. The neighbours must be nice. Philip said ______ invited him in for coffee ______ morning.

d) Don't worry – the new house will soon be ready. – He told me not to worry. He said the new house ______ soon be ready.

e) I'm going to get up very early. – He said ______ going to get up very early.

/ 5

5. **Complete the reported question.**

a) How long does the journey take?

I'd like to know how long ______________________________

b) Where's the nearest go-kart track?

I'm going to ask Mrs Taylor where ______________________________

c) They said: What do you think about it?

Yes, that's right, they asked me what ______________________________

d) How much did you pay for your stereo?

She asked me how much ______________________________

e) When is the next race?

I'd like to know when ______________________________

__ / 5

6. **Mark (↓) the right place for the word in brackets.**

a) Sandra's dad has been working since 1998. (at the post office)

b) Sandra eats meat. (never)

c) Sandra's little brother reads all day. (comics)

d) Sandra's mum is busy at the weekends. (usually)

e) Sandra writes to her penfriend every month. (an e-mail)

__ / 5

=======

__ / 30

Test 3 – Kapitel 13, 14, 18, 20, 21, 23

Bedingungssätze Typ I, II und III, indirekte Fragen, Gerundium und Infinitiv, modale Hilfsverben

1. **Complete the sentences with type I or II conditionals. Take the missing verb from the second sentence.**

a) If Mrs Black ____________________ us a vocabulary test on Monday, I ____________________ probably fail it. And she usually gives us a vocabulary test on Mondays. Oh dear!

b) Mrs Black ________________ (have) a shock if she ____________________ into the classroom now. But she never comes in at break time.

c) If our teacher _______ n't ___________ us such difficult tests, our marks ____________________ (be) better. But she gives us really difficult tests.

d) Becky copied from Karen in the test. Mrs Black ____________________ (be) angry if she ____________________. She usually notices if somebody has copied from someone else.

/ 8

2. **Complete the sentences. They are type II and type III conditionals.**

a) I waited for Michele this morning and so I missed the bus.

If I __________n't ______________________ for Michele, I __________n't _________________________________ the bus.

b) Karen doesn't eat any sweets, so she's quite thin.

If she ___________________ sweets, she ___________________ fatter.

c) Karen and Michele don't like each other, so it isn't easy for me.

It ___________________ easier for me if Karen and Michele ___________________ each other.

d) You didn't tell me about Michele's birthday so of course I didn't buy her a present.

If you ______________________ me, I ______________________

her a present.

e) Michele lives on the other side of the city, so I don't visit her very often.

I ______________________ her more often if she ______________

__________ so far away.

/ 10

3. Complete the sentences with the to-infinitive.

a) Robert: "Wait!" Robert told us ______________________________.

b) Frank: "What shall I draw?" Frank didn't know ____________________.

c) Robert: "Which DVD player shall I buy?"

Robert wasn't sure ______________________________________.

d) Frank: "Will you close the door, please?"

Frank asked me ______________________________________.

/ 4

4. Complete the sentences with the gerund or the infinitive of the verb in brackets.

a) James insists on ______________ his teeth after every meal. (clean)

b) He thinks if he stops ______________ it he will get caries. (do)

c) He remembers ______________ to the dentist when he was little. (go)

d) It wasn't much fun, so now he never forgets ______________ his teeth. (brush)

/ 4

5. **Frau Raab has just given a test back to her English class. What does she say? Complete the sentences with the modal auxiliaries in the box. There is one extra word, which you don't need.**

can't | needn't | might | mustn't | must

a) You ______ bring it back on or before the sixth of February.

b) If you've got a one or a two, you ______ get it signed by your parents, but everything from three to six has to be signed.

c) I need that test back, so you really ______ lose it!

d) If you don't bring them back, I ______ give you the next one to take home. I'll have to keep it.

___ / 4

=======

___ / 30

Test 4 – Kapitel 29 bis 33

Amerikanisches und britisches Englisch; Rechtschreibung, „vor", „gern" u. a. im Englischen; Übersetzungstraining

1. Find the correct German translation for the American words.

a) fall ______

b) elevator ______

c) neat ______

d) vacation ______

e) bathroom ______

/ 6 *f)* store ______

Aufzug
Badezimmer
Falle
Ferien
Herbst
Impfung
in Ordnung
Kaufladen
Lager
nett
Raumschiff
Toilette
Vorhang

2. Lucy received an e-mail from Anthony, whose hometown is Chicago, and another from Barrie, who is Welsh. Who wrote the questions below? Label each sentence A or B.

a) How many square meters is your new apartment? A ☐ B ☐

b) What colour are you going to paint the bathroom? A ☐ B ☐

c) Did you see that program about old houses on TV? A ☐ B ☐

d) Is your new place near the centre of town? A ☐ B ☐

e) Do you still have to travel twenty kilometres to work? A ☐ B ☐

/ 6 *f)* Have you found the best way of traveling to work? A ☐ B ☐

3. Complete the translations.

a) Warte vor dem Theater auf mich.

Wait for me ______

b) Ich werde vor sieben sicher dort sein.

I'll definitely be there ______

c) Ich nehme den Bus, der um Viertel vor sieben ankommt.

I'm going to take the bus that arrives ______________________________

d) Vor zwei Tagen habe ich zwanzig Minuten auf den Bus warten müssen.

______________________________ I had to wait twenty minutes for the bus.

e) Ich wartete vor dem Fußballstadion.

I was waiting ______________________________ the football stadium.

f) Leider war es kurz vor dem Beginn eines wichtigen Spiels.

Unfortunately it was just ______________________________of an important match. / *6*

4. **Complete the translations.**

a) Tony? Ich versuchte, ihn anzurufen, aber anscheinend ist er nicht zu Hause.

Tony? I tried to ring him, but ______________________________at home.

b) Vermutlich ist er bei Sarah.

______________________________ he's at Sarah's.

c) Irgendwo habe ich bestimmt Sarahs Nummer.

______________________________ somewhere.

d) Hoffentlich kann ich sie finden.

______________________________ find it.

e) Tony redet gern mit Sarah.

Tony ______________________________ to Sarah.

f) Er kommt mit Jungen gut aus, aber er verbringt seine Zeit lieber mit Mädchen.
He gets on well with boys, but he ______________________________
his time with girls. / *6*

5. **Underline the correct alternative.**

a) Anne is looking for a flat. She has informed herself / found out about a block of flats near the university.

b) But she's got a little daughter, and these flats don't seem very suitable for children / children friendly.

c) She was just going to / just wanted to sign the contract (Vertrag) when she realized that there was no playground.

d) Anne is a student. When she has finished at university / her study she's going to move back to Birmingham.

e) That's first / not until next summer.

/ 6 f) Luckily there are / it gives plenty of flats in Birmingham.

=======

/ 30

Test 5 – Kapitel 34 bis 36, 38, 41

„Falsche Freunde", Wörter im richtigen Zusammenhang verwenden, unregelmäßige Verben

1. **Tick the response which makes sense.**

a) Is Susan a brave girl?

A ☐ Oh, yes. She does everything she's told.
B ☐ Yes, she is. She once chased a thief out of her bedroom.

b) Did you pass the exam?

A ☐ No, I'll have to take it again.
B ☐ No, thank goodness.

c) Is your teacher very strong?

A ☐ I don't think so. She always asks us to carry books for her.
B ☐ No, not really. She doesn't say anything if we're late for school.

d) Does your mum control your homework?

A ☐ No, of course not. The teachers decide what we should do.
B ☐ No, not any more. She says I have to take more responsibility for myself.

e) Did you bring the map?

A ☐ Yes, all the papers are in it.
B ☐ Yes, I did. I don't know the way.

f) Why did you buy this bucket?

A ☐ No special reason. I just love flowers.
B ☐ My old one is broken and it doesn't hold water any more.

☐ / 6

2. **Complete the translations.**

a) Auf welcher Note stehe ich in Englisch?

What ______________________ have I got in English at the moment?

b) Was sind deine Lieblingschips? Meine sind cheese-and-onion.

What are your favourite _______________? Mine are cheese and onion.

c) Die Hälfte des Gelds haben wir gesammelt, die andere Hälfte wurde gespendet.
We collected half of the money ourselves,

the other half was ______________________________________.

d) Denk dran, dein Handy mitzunehmen.

Don't forget to take your ____________________________ with you.

e) Eine Piccoloflöte ist eine Art Querflöte.

A piccolo is a(n) ___________________________________ of flute.

f) Hast du die Kinokarten reserviert?

/ 6 Have you reserved the cinema ______________________________?

3. **Put the right word in the gap.**

a) Hals:

Have you got a sore ______________________? Have a cough sweet.

OK, go climbing, but don't break your _________________________!

b) ich bin fertig:

____________________________. Can I hand my test paper in now?

We can go now. __________________________, I've got my coat on.

c) Tasche/n:

These jeans have got five __________________________________.

/ 6 You have to leave your ________________________ in a locker before you go into the library.

4. **Add the correct particle from the box. There is one extra word.**

after – down – forward – off – out – up – up

a) We look ______ to hearing from you soon.

b) Don't look ______ every word in the dictionary. It will slow you down.

c) William? He rode his bike far too fast and fell ______.

d) Roger ran well at first, but then he fell ______.

e) My dad is picking me ______ after the party.

f) We can find ______ about ticket prices on the Internet.

___ / 6

5. **Choose a verb from the box and add the simple past and the past participle in the gaps.**

draw – ride – speak

a) Pierre only ______ French when he was little, but he hasn't ______ much French for years now.

b) Who ______ this picture? It's brilliant. – I think it was ______ by one of the students in Year 10.

c) Have you ever ______ a camel? – Yes, I have. We went to Egypt last year on holiday and we all ______ camels.

___ / 6

___ / 30

Lösungen zu den Übungen

6/7 **1** ***Zustandsverben (stative verbs)***

1. Korrigiere die Fehler.
a) I'm sorry, but I don't understand you.
b) Do you need anything for the journey?
c) we preferred to walk.
d) The sound seemed to get nearer.
e) This ring belonged / used to belong to my grandmother.

2. Ergänze *can / can't / could / couldn't* und *hear / see / smell* in jedem Satz. Der Inhalt sagt dir, welche Zeitform und welches Verb zu nehmen ist.
a) can't hear; *b)* could smell; *c)* can smell; *d)* could see; can't see

3. Unterstreiche die richtige Alternative.
a) I'm having; *b)* thinks; *c)* had; just having; *d)* I don't think

8/9 **2** ***Wiederholung der Zeitformen: past simple und past progressive***

1. Setze die Verben in Klammern in das *past progressive* oder *simple past.*
a) phoned; was just cleaning; *b)* was getting; called;
c) arrived; was just leaving; *d)* rang; was making

2. Verwende die Bilder und die Wörter im Kasten, um die Sätze zu vervollständigen.
a) was carrying; *b)* was sunbathing; *c)* wasn't looking; *d)* were working;
e) was writing

10/11 **3** ***Wiederholung der Zeitformen: present perfect simple und progressive***

1. Vervollständige die Sätze mit *since* + Zeitpunkt und *for* + Zeitraum. Schreibe wahre Sätze über dich. Für Satz *d)* wähle ein eigenes Verb.
individuelle Lösungen

2. Setze das Verb ins *present perfect simple* oder *progressive*.
a) have been playing; *b)* Have they ever played; *c)* hasn't been practising;
d) has just done; *e)* have started

3. **Finde eine Erklärung für diese Sätze.**
a) Yes, I've been working hard. *b)* I've been shouting.
c) I've just remembered something. *d)* I've been making bread.
e) She's been trying to feed herself again.

4 *Wiederholung der Zeitformen: will future und going to future* 12/13

1. **Bilde Sätze mit *will*.**
a) The bus will probably be late. *b)* Will you open the window, please?
c) The letter probably won't arrive until Friday.
d) What will he do?

2. **Bilde Sätze mit *going to.***
a) I'm certainly not going to go out in this weather.
b) It's going to rain.
c) Where is Anne going to have her baby?
d) Which piece are you going to play?

3. **Bilde Sätze mit *will* oder *going to*.**
a) it'll be / it will be; *b)* Is it going to rain? *c)* you'll pass;
d) probably won't have; *e)* isn't going to send; *f)* they're going to watch

5 *Wiederholung der Zeitformen: simple past und present perfect* 14/15

1. **Setze das Verb in das *simple past.***
didn't agree; left; wanted; thought; were; was; made; didn't land; came; started; survived; spoke; taught; became

2. **Setze das Verb in das *present perfect.***
has been; has always had; have made; have written; has been

3. **Setze das Verb in das *simple past* oder *present perfect.***
came; didn't possess; managed; have been; took over; have made; have risen; started; thought; didn't know

6 *Aktiv und Passiv I* 16/17

1. **Mache aus den Passivsätzen Aktivsätze und behalte die Zeitform bei.**
a) Volunteers have decorated the old people's home.
b) A neighbour drove the two girls home.
c) the bride's mother will make the wedding dress.

2. Bilde Passivsätze aus diesen Aktivsätzen.
Der Handelnde „verschwindet" aus dem Passivsatz.
a) Criminals are usually caught eventually.
b) This silver spoon is only used on special occasions.
c) This photo was taken last Christmas.

3. Unterstreiche die richtige Alternative.
a) is given; *b)* gets; *c)* have never been worn; *d)* been eaten; *e)* are picked; *f)* watched; *g)* was watched; *h)* been lit; *i)* was stopped; *j)* stopped

18/19

7 Aktiv und Passiv II

1. Diese Sätze enthalten typische deutsche Fehler.
Verwandle sie in Passivsätze. Achte auf die Zeitformen.
a) The magazine is written by the pupils.
b) This house was built by my grandfather.
c) The voice-over in the film was done by a boy at our school.
d) The steps are cleaned by the children.

2. Setze das Verb in Klammern in die aktive oder passive Form des *simple present.*
a) is taken; *b)* usually cook; *c)* are often done; *d)* is read; *e)* rises

3. Setze das Verb in Klammern in die aktive oder passive Form des *simple past.*
a) was stolen; *b)* made; *c)* gave; *d)* was given

4. Bilde Aktiv- oder Passivsätze aus diesen Kombinationen aus Hilfsverb und Verb.
a) must be done; *b)* mustn't be seen; *c)* needn't finish;
d) should be switched off; *e)* must lock

20/21

8 Passivsätze mit zwei Objekten

1. Schreibe die Aktivsätze zu diesen Passivsätzen.
Verwende *they*, falls es keinen *by-agent* gibt.
a) My parents have promised me a new bike.
b) They told us a lot of stories which we didn't believe.
c) I hope they will offer my dad the job.
d) Have they given you more time for the project?
e) Susan Adams has given me your address.

2. **Und nun das Gleiche andersrum.**
Du brauchst keinen *by-agent* bei *they* oder *somebody*.
a) Mandy has been promised a trekking holiday by her parents.
b) We have been sent a brochure about adventure holidays.
c) Yesterday Tim and Susan were offered free tickets for the circus.
d) At the museum we were shown some old film sets.
e) The girls were shown some photographs of the race.

9 *Passiv bei Objekten mit Präposition* 22/23

1. **Unterstreiche das Subjekt und die Präposition, die dazugehört, in jedem dieser Passivsätze.**
a) The Queen – about; *b)* Vegetarians – for; *c)* Churches – in

2. **Als Matthews Eltern nach einem Wochenende auswärts zurückkamen, stellten sie fest, dass ihr Haus für eine Party genutzt wurde. Stelle die einzelnen Teile der Sätze in die richtige Reihenfolge.**
a) Matthew's bed hadn't been slept in.
b) The table had been danced on.
c) The flower beds had been trodden on.
d) The garden hose had been played with.

3. **Bilde Passivsätze.**
a) have been played with; *b)* has been slept in; *c)* has been trodden on; *d)* has been drunk out of; *e)* have been swept under; *f)* have been looked after

10 *Past perfect I* 24/25

1. **Dieser Text beginnt Sonntagnachmittag. Unterstreiche die Verben von allem, was davor geschah.**
had played; had lost; had done; had taken; *a)* past perfect; *b)* simple past

2. **Dieser Text beginnt Viertel vor acht an einem Montagmorgen.**
a) had forgotten; had arrived; *b)* past perfect

3. **Verwende verschiedene Farben, um zu unterstreichen, was *a)* vor und *b)* nach dem Ereignis im ersten Satz geschah.**
a) had quietly walked; hadn't noticed;
b) looked round; saw him; didn't know; just smiled; went

4. Schau jeden dieser Kurztexte genau an und entscheide, welches Ereignis zuerst geschah, welches als nächstes und so weiter. Dann schreibe die Buchstaben in der chronologischen Reihenfolge hin.
a) BAC; *b)* ACB; *c)* ACB; *d)* CAB

26/27

11 Past perfect II

1. Hier ist eine kleine Geschichte. Lies sie und verwende das *past perfect*, um die Reihenfolge zu ändern.
Topple and Co were asked to make a fence at Oakland old folks' home, because the people there had wanted a fence round the garden for years. They made a bad mistake because they hadn't planned the fence very well. After they had finished the fence, they found that they couldn't get their lorry out.

2. Barney ist nicht sehr schlau. Erkläre ihm diese Witze mit einem Satz im *past perfect.*
a) Mrs Noah had cooked the other one.
b) she had eaten it.
c) she had burnt the chair.

28/29

12 Wiederholung der Zeitformen: past progressive und past perfect (progressive)

1. Kreuze den richtigen Satz an, der zum Zusammenhang passt.
a) The last sentence was very long and complicated.
b) I had to wait.
c) He asked Pete to fetch him a spanner.
d) We were sorry about missing him.

2. Setze das Verb ins *past progressive* oder *past perfect.*
a) had written
b) was looking for; had used
c) was just going
d) had forgotten
e) was waiting

3. Unterstreiche die richtige Form des Verbs: *past perfect progressive* oder *past progressive.*
a) had been running; *b)* had been watching; *c)* was bathing; *d)* had been sitting on

13 Bedingungssätze Typ I und Typ II

30/31

1. Setze den *if*-Satz ein, verwende dabei das Verb aus dem zweiten Satz. Eines der Verben ist verneint.
a) If Sandra phones; *b)* If that book doesn't come soon; *c)* If I manage

2. Bedingungssätze des Typs II für irreale Situationen in der Gegenwart. Setze den *if*-Satz ein und verwende dabei den *but*-Satz für die Informationen, die du brauchst.
a) If I was rich / If I were rich; *b)* If Steve didn't smoke so much;
c) If this train stopped at every station

3. Bedingungssätze des Typs II für unwahrscheinliche Ereignisse in der Zukunft. Verwende den zweiten Satz für die Informationen, die du benötigst.
a) If I won the jackpot; *b)* if you saw a ghost; *c)* If the school caught fire

14 Bedingungssätze Typ III

32/33

1. Schreibe den *if*-Satz zu diesen Sätzen. Verwende die unterstrichenen Elemente für die benötigten Informationen. Der *would*-Satz steht im *present*.
a) If Richard hadn't lived in Italy
b) If Wendy hadn't bought an electric piano
c) If they had put their coats on

2. Verwende die unterstrichenen Teile, um *if*-Sätze zu bilden. Diesmal ist der *would*-Satz in der Vergangenheit.
a) If I hadn't studied hard; *b)* If I hadn't gone to the party;
c) If you had looked under the doormat

3. Beende den Satz mit einem *would have*- oder *wouldn't have*-Satz, verwende dabei die Vorschläge in den Boxen.
a) I would have gone to the party
b) the boys would have woken up
c) we wouldn't have missed our connection
d) he would have caught the plane

34/35 15 *Indirekte Rede (reported speech)*

1. **Einige Teile von Text A sind unterstrichen. Unterstreiche die gleichen Teile in Text B.**

Alan is telling his friend Philip about the letter.

See this? It's a letter to my mum from my uncle in Australia. He says he's sure that I would like to visit him on his farm again. He says I can go out there next summer if my mum agrees, and that Peter can come too if he wants to. He says he'll meet us both at the airport. He tried to phone my mum the week before, but he couldn't get through.

2. **Kannst du herausfinden, was Alan eigentlich sagt?**

Alan: I sometimes visit my uncle in Australia. My uncle meets us in Melbourne. Then we have a long drive to his sheep farm. You've met my uncle. Don't you remember?

3. **Jetzt bist du dran zu berichten.**

Alan says they have great fun on the farm. He says they often ride their uncle's horses. They ride around the fence with him. He says he'll send me a postcard from Australia, but he doesn't know when it will get here.

36/37 16 *Reported speech in der Vergangenheit*

1. **Dieser Text ist in der indirekten Rede geschrieben. Was hat Alan tatsächlich gesagt?**

Alan: Hello, Phil. It's me. I'm still in Australia. Something terrible has happened here. My uncle is in hospital and he can't take us to the airport, so we'll probably miss our plane.

2. **Jetzt kannst du die Unterhaltung in die indirekte Rede übertragen.**

Philip is telling his friends about the phone call.

He said he could tell me exactly what had happened, but that it would take a long time, because it was a long story. He asked me if I wanted to hear it. I said I did, but that his uncle would have to pay a lot for the phone call. I told him to tell me when he got home. Then Alan said that his uncle had had a bad accident the day before. He said that he had broken his leg and that he wouldn't be able to ride a horse for a few weeks. He said he wanted to stay there with Peter, so that they could help their uncle on the farm, but he said he didn't think his mother would let them.

17 Fragen in der indirekten Rede

38/39

1. **Wie lautet die Frage?**
   a) How old are you, Paul?
   b) Where can I leave my bags?
   c) What does 'weather' mean?
   d) When do the holidays start?
   e) Where's the ticket office?
   f) When does the next ferry leave for the Isle of Wight?

2. **Jetzt bist du dran, die indirekten Fragen zu vervollständigen. Vergiss nicht die Zeitformen zurückzusetzen und die Pronomen zu ändern.**
   a) where you've put your bike.
   b) how old this church is, please?
   c) how much the pullover cost.
   d) where we can swim.
   e) what I had done with the money.

18 Indirekte Fragen mit dem to-Infinitiv

40/41

1. **Bilde direkte Fragen mit *shall* aus diesen indirekten Fragen mit *to*.**
   a) Where shall we go?
   b) What shall I wear?
   c) When shall I leave?
   d) Which basketball shall I buy?
   e) Which way shall we go?
   f) What shall I do with it?
   g) Who shall I give it to?

2. **Bringe diese Wörter in die richtige Reihenfolge, um indirekte Fragen mit dem *to*-Infinitiv zu bilden.**
   a) Sarah doesn't know what to do.
   b) I don't know when to post it.
   c) I don't know which one to buy.

3. **Jetzt bist du dran, indirekte Fragen mit dem *to*-Infinitiv zu bilden.**
   a) what to cook.
   b) how to repair a bike chain.
   c) which animals to feed.
   d) which plants to water.
   e) how to switch the computer off.
   f) what to do.

19 Indirekte Aufforderungen mit dem to-Infinitiv

42/43

1. **Schreibe die direkte Version dieser indirekten Anweisungen.**
   a) Wait, please.
   b) Empty your pockets, please.
   c) Will you phone me at six o'clock, please?

2. **Schreibe die direkte Version dieser indirekten, verneinten Bitten.**
a) Please don't smoke here.
b) Don't forget Dad's birthday.
c) Don't bother (to get me a chair).

3. **Jetzt bist du dran eine indirekte Fassung zu schreiben. Vergiss nicht die Pronomen zu ändern, wo es notwendig ist. Dies sagte der Englischlehrer:**
a) not to waste time.
b) to stop playing with my ruler.
c) to put it away.
d) told Group A to turn to page 52 … to turn to page 106.
e) to work with a partner from the other group and to follow the instructions.
f) not to look at our partner's information.
g) told us to look up any new words in the dictionary.

44/45

20 *Gerundium und Infinitiv I*

1. **Übersetze ins Englische und verwende dabei die folgenden Ausdrücke.**
a) I'm interested in riding.
b) The teacher insists on keeping all the windows closed / shut.
c) Tom and his friends apologized for making so much noise.
d) Thanks for waiting for me!

2. **Verwende die Verben in Klammern im Infinitiv oder als Gerundium.**
a) to go; *b)* taking; *c)* to ride; *d)* to lend; *e)* discussing; *f)* to borrow; *g)* to be; *h)* seeing; *i)* riding; *j)* going

46/47

21 *Gerundium und Infinitiv II*

1. **Vervollständige die deutschen Übersetzungen. In den meisten Fällen wirst du einen dieser Ausdrücke benötigen.**
a) singt gern
b) fing an
c) macht … lieber
d) tanzen sehr gern;
e) rennt sehr ungern
f) störte weiterhin

2. **Wähle die passende Ergänzung zu den Sätzen.**
a) B; *b)* A; *c)* A; *d)* A; *e)* A; *f)* B

22 *Stellung der Adverbien* 48/49

1. **Unterstreiche das Adverb / die adverbiale Bestimmung in jedem dieser Sätze. Zeichne einen Kreis um das Verb und Objekt.**
   a) twice a week; buys fresh vegetables; *b)* sometimes; cooks a meal; *c)* very well; make shepherd's pie; *d)* At the weekend; makes a pizza or spaghetti bolognaise; *e)* often; invites her best friend

2. **Markiere die richtige Stellung für das Adverb in Klammern.**
   a) Ben plays football **very well**.
   b) He's playing football **now**.
   c) He doesn't **usually** play football on **Saturdays**.
   d) But there's an important match **today**.
   e) He **never** misses a match.

3. **Unterstreiche die adverbiale Bestimmung des Ortes in jedem dieser Sätze.**
   a) to the cinema; *b)* at a fast food place; *c)* home; *d)* to bed

4. **Markiere die richtige Stellung im Satz von jedem Wort oder Ausdruck in Klammern.**
   a) Maxi sits **at his computer** until late at night.
   b) He surfs **the Internet** for hours.
   c) His mum has stopped sending him **to bed** at night.
   d) These days, she goes **to bed** before him.
   e) In the morning he's supposed to leave **the house** at seven thirty.
   f) As you can imagine, he often comes **to school** late.

5. **Ordne die Satzelemente in der richtigen Reihenfolge an. Die Johnsons gehen in Urlaub. Mutter erzählt Adam, wie das Auto zu packen ist.**
   a) Put the big things in the boot first.
   b) Then put the smaller things in the spaces afterwards.
   c) The coats go right on top when we've finished.
   d) Take the sandwiches out of the fridge just before we leave.

23 *Modale Hilfsverben* 50/51

1. **Finde ein passendes englisches Hilfsverb für jeden dieser deutschen Sätze.**
   a) might; *b)* can't; *c)* can; *d)* should; *e)* needn't; *f)* mustn't

2. **Bilde Paare aus Sätzen, die zusammengehören, indem du sie mit Pfeilen verbindest.**
   a) You must walk to school. – You're overweight.
   You have to walk to school. – There isn't a bus.
   b) I'm not allowed to waste time. – My mum is very strict about that.
   I mustn't waste any time. – I want to watch the Simpsons.
   c) You needn't do the washing up. – You're in a hurry, so I'll do it.
   You don't have to do the washing up. – Lucky you!
   d) We shouldn't smoke here. – I don't want to upset the non-smokers.
   We aren't supposed to smoke here. – It's a silly rule.

3. **Stelle die Wörter in die richtige Reihenfolge.**
   a) He can't have gone far.
   b) She might have left us a note.
   c) You could easily have got lost.
   d) It may have been brought in by the cat.

52/53

24 Texte lesen und verstehen

1. **Lies den Text. Du musst nicht alles verstehen, um die Aufgabe zu bearbeiten.**

2. **Mache einen Haken bei „richtig" oder „falsch" zu jeder Aussage über den Text.**
   a) wrong (stars)
   b) wrong (the early hours of the morning)
   c) right (more stars than I had ever seen)
   d) right (literally dozens)
   e) wrong (must have been … but I didn't know about such things then)
   f) right (mid-August)
   g) wrong (my mind was too occupied)

3. **Wähle die richtige Alternative.**
   a) towards
   b) pleased with himself
   c) a previous conversation

4. **Beantworte die Fragen zum Text in ganzen Sätzen. Verwende die vorgegebenen Satzanfänge.**
   a) The writer is impressed by the brightness of the stars in the cloudless sky.
   b) We know that the writer is not familiar with the area because he thinks that it 'must always be like this'. This is obviously his first summer in the area.
   c) In the first line, we read that the writer is going 'drunkenly' home, implying that he is rather drunk / has been drinking alcohol.

25 Notizen für einen Text anfertigen 54/55

1. **Lies die Notizen und unterstreiche die richtige Alternative.**
   with; or; on; between; suffers; every; is caused by; of course

2. **Lies die Notizen und vervollständige den Text mit den vorgegebenen Wörtern.**
   Hurricane – on – begun – in – reached – hurricane – or – of – However

3. **Verwende die Notizen, um den Text fortzusetzen. Vergleiche dann deinen Text mit der Musterlösung im hinteren Teil des Buches. Du kannst Wörter ändern.**
   A **total** of 23 people in the US and three **more** in the Bahamas **died** in the hurricane. $26.5 billion of damage was caused, most of **it** in south Florida. Since 1992 the measuring equipment and early warning systems for hurricanes **have been** improved. Consequently, the population **should be** better prepared for the **next** hurricane.

26 Informationen sinnvoll anordnen 56/57

1. **Unterstreiche die Informationen über Nahrungsmittel in den drei Blöcken von Notizen.**
   a) **Christmas Eve:** preparation of food; last-minute shopping; stockings hung up; no special meal.
   Christmas Day: presents opened round tree, big meal, lazy afternoon, lots of sweets.
   b) **Christmas Eve:** shops open late, food bought, perhaps midnight mass, Santa Claus / chimney.
   Christmas Day: children unpack stockings (traditionally fruit and nuts, nowadays chocolate and other presents), no shops open, church in the morning, turkey and Christmas pudding, paper hats and crackers.

c) **Advent:** advent calendar, often with a sweet for each day; no special church events.
Christmas Eve: increasing excitement, everyone busy with last-minute preparations; shops very busy, especially sale of turkeys.
Christmas Day: children up at dawn to open stockings – probably eating sweets from stocking before breakfast; mothers spend morning in the kitchen preparing meal; turkey with vegetables and sauces, wine, followed by Christmas pudding. Afternoon walk or watching TV.

2. **Du hältst einen Vortrag mit zwei anderen über Weihnachten in Amerika. Dein Thema ist Essen. Verbinde die unterstrichenen Teile von oben, um einen zusammenhängenden Text zu schreiben.**
Lösungsvorschlag: In America food plays a very important role in the Christmas festivities. It starts at the beginning of December, as most advent calendars contain sweets. There is no special meal on Christmas Eve, but the day is largely spent buying and preparing food for the next day, especially the turkey. On Christmas Day the eating starts before breakfast, with the children unpacking and eating chocolate from their stockings. Traditionally, the stockings contain fruit and nuts, but these have been replaced by sweets. The big meal of the day is at midday, with roast turkey, vegetables and sauces. The adults drink wine. After the turkey comes the Christmas pudding. After dinner the eating continues, as a lot of sweets are eaten.

58/59

27 *Textproduktion*

1. **Lies den Text.**

2. **Die Geschichte ist aus Lucys Perspektive geschrieben. Stelle dir vor, du bist der Faun. Schreibe einen Brief an einen Freund über das Treffen mit Lucy. Vergiss nicht die Einleitung und ein passendes Ende.**
Dear Tilly,
Thank you for your letter. It was wonderful to hear from you again.
You asked me what I had been doing recently. Well, life has been boring – at least, until a strange experience the other day. I was going home through the woods when I met a Daughter of Eve – a real human. She told me she came from the city of War Drobe in Spare Oom. I've never heard of those places. Have you? Anyway, she said that in Spare Oom it is summer. Imagine it! Here it has been winter for so long. I was very interested, so I invited her to tea. So you see, there really are humans. You thought they didn't really exist, didn't you?
I hope you're well and look forward to seeing you soon, Tumi

28 *Wortfeld: Geschichte Amerikas* 60/61

1. **In jeder Gruppe ist ein Wort, das nicht passt. Unterstreiche das unpassende Wort.**

a) Inuit (die einzigen hier aufgelisteten Eingeborenen)
b) Silicon Valley (die einzige moderne Erscheinung)
c) prairie (das Einzige, das nicht zur Stadt gehört)

2. **Versuche das Kreuzworträtsel zu vervollständigen.**

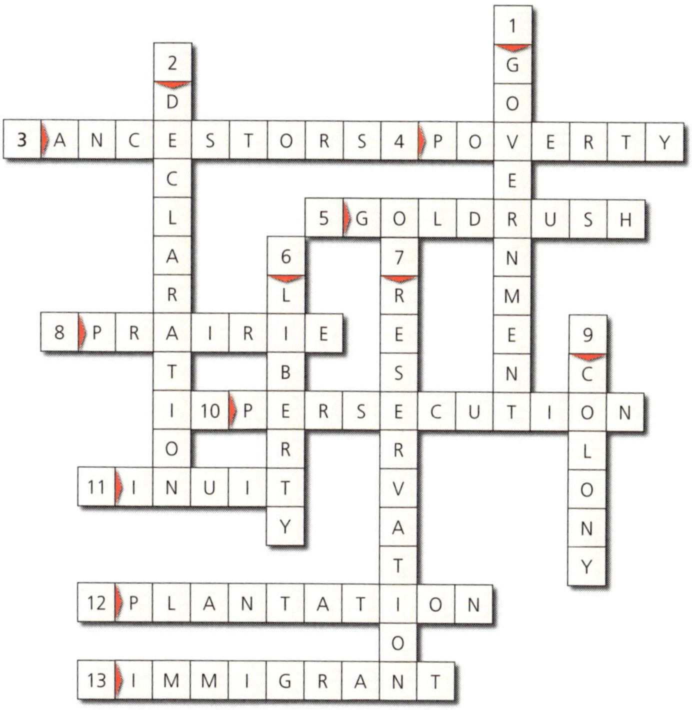

29 *Amerikanisches und britisches Englisch* 62/63

1. **Finde die sinnvollste Alternative zu jedem Satz im amerikanischen Englisch.**

a) be in the tenth grade; *b)* baby buggy; *c)* is fun; *d)* relax …; *e)* 4th October

2. **Kristin ist Amerikanerin. Sie ist gerade bei der älteren Mrs. Barton, einer britischen Dame, die nie amerikanische Filme schaut oder amerikanische Bücher liest. Hilf ihnen bei ihren Missverständnissen.**

a) the pupils; *b)* the toilet; *c)* the first floor; *d)* zed

64/65 **30** *Besonderheiten der Rechtschreibung im amerikanischen Englisch*

1. Bezeichne die folgenden Sätze als amerikanisches Englisch (AE) oder britisches Englisch (BE).
a) BE; *b)* BE; *c)* AE; *d)* AE; *e)* AE

2. Wähle die richtige Alternative, um britisches und amerikanisches Englisch nicht zu vermischen.
a) theatre; *b)* centre; *c)* kilometers

3. Finde die amerikanische Schreibweise in jeder Gruppe.
a) honor; *b)* meters; *c)* harbor; *d)* traveling

66/67 **31** *Übersetzungsmöglichkeiten für „vor"*

1. Unterstreiche mögliche Wörter, die zum Kontext passen. Es können mehr als eins sein.
a) the house; the class
b) the camera; the teacher
c) the concert; the end of term
d) winter; sunset

2. Unterstreiche das richtige Wort für den Kontext. Nur eins ist richtig.
a) ago; *b)* to; *c)* in front of; *d)* before

3. Übersetze ins Deutsche.
a) Quentins Schwester ging vor zwei Jahren nach Amerika.
b) Quentin wohnte zwei Monate bei seiner Schwester in New York.

4. Finde den richtigen Kontext für jeden Satz.
a) B; *b)* B; *c)* A

68/69 **32** *„Gern", „hoffentlich" etc. auf Englisch*

1. Verbinde die englischen und deutschen Sätze.
bestimmt – I'm sure; vermutlich – I expect; anscheinend – seems; hoffentlich – I hope

2. Übersetze ins Deutsche. Verwende die vorgegebenen Wörter.
a) Ich klettere gern. *b)* Hoffentlich bleibt das Wetter schön.
c) Anscheinend hast du Angst. *d)* Du fällst bestimmt nicht.
e) Würdest du mir lieber beim Klettern zuschauen?

3. **Frau Weber vermietet eine Ferienwohnung an eine englische Familie. Sie hat eine Nachricht auf dem Küchentisch hinterlassen. Übersetze die kursiven Teile ins Englische.**
   a) I hope you had a good journey.
   b) I'm sure you're hungry after your journey.
   c) If you like walking
   d) But perhaps you prefer swimming.
   e) now it seems to be open every day.
   f) so I expect you'll have lots of sunshine.

33 *Übersetzungstraining* — 70/71

1. **Übersetze die Sätze mit dem vorgegebenen Vokabular.**
   a) Es lohnt sich, sich über Billigflüge zu informieren.
   b) Hochhäuser sind nicht besonders kinderfreundlich.
   c) Die meisten Leute lassen sich von Abfällen nicht stören.
   d) Helme sind Pflicht.
   e) David macht gerade ein Studium an der Universität.
   f) Die Jungen strengten sich an und es gelang ihnen, den Gipfel zu erreichen.
   g) Ramona hat vor, während der Fastenzeit auf Schokolade zu verzichten.

2. **Übersetze den folgenden Abschnitt. Entscheide, welche der Alternativen in Klammern zu verwenden ist.**
   Als ich meine Familie verließ, stellte ich mir alles einfach vor. Zu Hause waren wir sechs Kinder, meine Mutter hatte keine richtige Arbeit und meinen Vater hatten wir seit Wochen nicht mehr gesehen. Bevor ich die Hütte verließ, sagte ich meiner Mutter, ich wollte Arbeit suchen. Ich war schließlich der älteste Sohn. Aber es ist schwierig, Arbeit zu finden, wenn man erst elf Jahre alt ist.

34 *„Falsche Freunde" – Textverständnis* — 72/73

1. **Finde die richtige Übersetzung aus dem Kasten und schreibe sie auf die Schreiblinie.**
   a) Fußboden; *b)* Landkarte; *c)* bestehen; *d)* stark; *e)* beschuldigen; *f)* tapfer

2. **Wähle den passenden Kontext.**
   a) B; *b)* B; *c)* A; *d)* A; *e)* B; *f)* B; *g)* A; *h)* B

74/75 35 *„Falsche Freunde" – Textproduktion*

1. Unterstreiche das richtige Wort.
a) murderer; *b)* kind; *c)* mobile; *d)* menu; *e)* bell

2. Unterstreiche den Fehler in jedem Satz und korrigiere ihn, indem du eines dieser Wörter verwendest. Du benötigst nicht alle Wörter.
a) chief ➟ boss; *b)* stall ➟ hutch; *c)* blame ➟ make a fool of;
d) brave ➟ good; *e)* spend ➟ give (auch: donate)

3. Vervollständige die Übersetzung, indem du einige Wörter aus dem Kasten verwendest.
a) mobiles; *b)* crisps; *c)* sort / kind; *d)* notes; *e)* mark

76/77 36 *Wörter im richtigen Zusammenhang verwenden*

1. Welches deutsche Wort passt zu beiden Bedeutungen?
a) schwer; *b)* Kissen; *c)* Hals; *d)* erinnern; *e)* andere; *f)* Preis;
g) fertig; *h)* Stunde; *i)* Tasche

2. Nenne das richtige englische Wort für das deutsche Wort in Klammern.
a) bag; *b)* prize; *c)* have finished; *d)* lessons; *e)* Remind; *f)* throat;
g) pillow; *h)* difficult; *i)* another

78/79 37 *Feste Wendungen im Englischen*

1. Übersetze die unterstrichenen Teile ins Deutsche.
a) aus heiterem Himmel; *b)* außer; *c)* weit; *d)* natürlich; *e)* allein

2. Unterstreiche die richtige Alternative.
a) a; *b)* to; *c)* to; *d)* on; *e)* at; *f)* it

3. Finde ein Wort im Kasten für jede Lücke.
Es gibt einige zusätzliche Wörter, die du nicht brauchen wirst.
a) in; *b)* thank; *c)* goes; *d)* stores; *e)* matter;
f) left; *g)* short; *h)* says; *i)* in

38 *Phrasal verbs* 80/81

1. **Übersetze die folgenden Sätze ins Deutsche.**

a) **Freust** du dich auf die Party?

b) Wenn du ein Wort nicht kennst, kannst du es im Wörterbuch **nachschlagen**.

c) Darren läuft auf den Händen, aber schau nicht hin. Er **gibt** nur **an**.

d) Hier sind die Farben. **Suche** diejenigen Farben **aus**, die du brauchst.

e) Ich will Krankenschwester werden, aber ich weiß nicht, welche Prüfungen ich bestehen muss. – Dann **informiere dich**.

2. **Unterstreiche die richtige Alternative.**

a) through; *b)* on; *c)* up; *d)* up; *e)* on

3. **Füge die richtigen Partikel aus dem Kasten ein. Ein Wort ist zusätzlich.**

a) forward; *b)* after; *c)* out; *d)* around; *e)* down

4. **Füge ein passendes Wort in der *-ing* Form in jeden Satz ein.**

a) seeing; *b)* listening; *c)* reading; *d)* going; *e)* (z.B. I'm looking forward to going skiing at the weekend.)

39 *Mengen- und Zeitangaben in Aussagesätzen und Fragen / Verneinungen* 82/83

1. **Setze ein ...**

a) a long way; *b)* a long time; *c)* a long way; *d)* a lot; *e)* a long time; *f)* A lot of

2. **Setze ein ... Der Stil ist förmliches Schriftenglisch.**

a) a long time; *b)* long; *c)* a long time; *d)* a long time

3. **Setze ein ... Der Stil ist förmliches Schriftenglisch.**

a) far; *b)* a long way; *c)* a long way

4. **Setze ein ... Der Stil ist förmliches Schriftenglisch.**

a) a lot of; *b)* a lot of; *c)* much; *d)* a lot of

84/85 ## 40 *Unregelmäßige Verben I: simple past*

1. Schreibe den Infinitiv zu diesen *simple past* Formen.
a) feel; *b)* drive; *c)* eat; *d)* read; *e)* fall; *f)* wear; *g)* sleep

2. Schreibe die *simple past* Form zu diesen Infinitiven.
a) chose; *b)* sold; *c)* wrote; *d)* went; *e)* took; *f)* spent; *g)* understood

3. Ergänze das *simple past* oder den Infinitiv des Verbs in Klammern.
a) ran; *b)* win; *c)* lost; *d)* got; *e)* swim; *f)* went

4. Markiere die *simple past* Formen. Es gibt elf davon.
told; shone; saw; caught; knew; meant; were; drove; held; bent; made

5. Finde die unpassende Form. Eine *simple past* Form reimt sich nicht mit den *simple past* Formen der anderen beiden Verben.
a) ring; *b)* feel; *c)* show; *d)* cast; *e)* draw; *f)* shut

86/87 ## 41 *Unregelmäßige Verben II: past participle*

1. Markiere die Verben, deren Partizip Perfekt von der *simple past* Form abweicht. Es gibt sieben davon.
ride; come; shake; go; eat; drink; grow

2. Nenne den Infinitiv dieser Partizip Perfekt Formen.
a) feel; *b)* fall; *c)* go; *d)* wear; *e)* speak

3. Nenne die Partizip Perfekt Formen dieser Infinitive.
a) been; *b)* chosen; *c)* ridden; *d)* done; *e)* hidden

4. Ergänze das *simple past* und das Partizip Perfekt des Verbs in Klammern.
a) did – done; *b)* drunk – drank; *c)* spoke – spoken

5. Ergänze das Partizip Perfekt eines passenden Verbs im Kasten. Es gibt ein zusätzliches Verb, das du nicht brauchst.
a) forgotten; *b)* drawn; *c)* seen; *d)* caught; *e)* shown; *f)* been

42 *Unregelmäßige Pluralformen* 88/89

1. **Nenne den Singular zu diesen Pluralformen.**
a) yourself; *b)* wife; *c)* knife; *d)* settler; *e)* litre

2. **Nenne den Singular zu diesen Pluralformen.**
a) goose; *b)* deer; *c)* woman; *d)* person; *e)* foot

3. **Nenne die Pluralform.**
a) lives; *b)* knives; *c)* scarves; *d)* thieves; *e)* computers; *f)* monsters; *g)* euros; *h)* kilometres; *i)* winters

4. **Nenne die Pluralform.**
a) men; *b)* children; *c)* teeth; *d)* sheep; *e)* mice; *f)* fish

5. **Vervollständige die Ausdrücke mit den vorgegebenen Wörtern.**
a) pound; *b)* hour; *c)* minute; *d)* page; *e)* litre; *f)* letter

43 *Wortfeld: Schule in den USA* 90/91

1. **In diesem Spiel musst du entscheiden, welches die richtige Definition oder das richtige Synonym ist. Unterstreiche das Richtige.**
a) school grounds; *b)* head of a school; *c)* exercise book; *d)* holiday; *e)* team representative; *f)* school timetable; *g)* a game with a ball

2. **Verbinde die amerikanischen Nomen mit den Erklärungen.**
a) grade; *b)* football; *c)* period; *d)* classes; *e)* student council; *f)* yearbook; *g)* diploma

3. **Annika hat Probleme mit dem amerikanischen Englisch. Vervollständige die Übersetzung.**
Brieffreundin – die Schule – den Ferien – in der zehnten Klasse – die Abschlussprüfung ablegen – Stundenplan – Stunden – Mathe – der amerikanische Fußball / Football – Fußball und Baseball

Lösungen zu den Tests

Notenschlüssel zu den Tests

Punktzahl:	30–29	28	27–25	24	23–21	20	19–16	15
Note:	1	1–2	2	2–3	3	3–4	4	4–5

92/93 **Test 1**

1. *a)* was having – have got *b)* thinks – isn't thinking

2. tried – picked up – were you doing – was playing – went

3. *a)* A: Doesn't it look nice?
   b) B: There are books all over the table.
   c) B: Oh, did she go to lots of parties last week?
   d) A: Auntie Mabel says we can stay with her in the summer holidays.
   e) B: I wish we were still there!

4. *a)* It's going to rain. *b)* the weather will be nice; *c)* are going to have; *d)* are going to take; *e)* is going to buy; *f)* will make

5. *a)* has made; *b)* has already eaten; *c)* stole; *d)* climbed; *e)* has never done

6. *a)* hadn't finished; *b)* was washing; *c)* had written; *d)* was reading; *e)* had gone

94/96 **Test 2**

1. *a)* were found; *b)* are written by; *c)* always eat; *d)* brought; *e)* hurts

2. *a)* The twins have been given new mobile phones by their uncle.
   b) This bed has already been slept in.
   c) The children are looked after by a neighbour every day.
   d) We were offered tea with milk.
   e) The visitors were shown round the house by a servant.

3. *a)* he is; *b)* she wants; *c)* his – mine; *d)* she – her; *e)* she hasn't – my

4. *a)* was watching; *b)* had put; *c)* they had – that; *d)* would; *e)* he was

5. *a)* the journey takes; *b)* the nearest go-kart track is; *c)* I thought about it; *d)* I had paid for my stereo; *e)* the next race is

6. *a)* has been working at the post office since 1998
b) Sandra never eats
c) reads comics all day
d) is usually busy
e) writes an e-mail to her penfriend

Test 3 97/99

1. *a)* gives – will; *b)* would have – came; *c)* didn't give – would be; *d)* will be – notices;

2. *a)* If I hadn't waited for Michele, I wouldn't have missed the bus.
b) If she ate sweets, she would be fatter.
c) It would be easier for me if Karen and Michele liked each other.
d) If you had told me, I would have bought her a present.
e) I would visit her more often if she didn't live so far away.

3. *a)* Robert told us to wait. *b)* Frank didn't know what to draw. *c)* Robert wasn't sure which DVD player to buy. *d)* Frank asked me to close the door.

4. *a)* cleaning; *b)* doing; *c)* going; *d)* to brush

5. *a)* must; *b)* needn't; *c)* mustn't; *d)* can't

Test 4 100/102

1. *a)* Herbst; *b)* Aufzug; *c)* nett; *d)* Ferien; *e)* Toilette; *f)* Kaufladen

2. *a)* A; *b)* B; *c)* A; *d)* B; *e)* B; *f)* A

3. *a)* in front of the theatre; *b)* before seven; *c)* at quarter to seven; *d)* Two days ago; *e)* in front of; *f)* before the beginning

4. *a)* he doesn't seem to be at home; *b)* I expect he's at Sarah's;
c) I'm sure I've got Sarah's number; *d)* I hope I can find it;
e) Tony likes talking to Sarah; *f)* prefers to spend / prefers spending

5. *a)* found out; *b)* suitable for children; *c)* was just going to;
d) at university; *e)* not until; *f)* there are

103/105 *Test 5*

1. *a)* B; *b)* A; *c)* A; *d)* A; *e)* B; *f)* B;

2. *a)* mark; *b)* crisps; *c)* donated; *d)* mobile / mobile phone; *e)* kind of / sort of;
f) tickets

3. *a)* throat – neck; *b)* I've finished – I'm ready; *c)* pockets – bags;

4. *a)* forward; *b)* up; *c)* off; *d)* down; *e)* up; *f)* out

5. *a)* spoke – spoken; *b)* drew – drawn; *c)* ridden – rode